Stiletto Chronicles: Stories from the Pole

Stiletto Chronicles: Stories from the Pole

Acknowledgments

Thank you to my daughter;
Without her I would not be.
I love you to the moon and back pumpkin pie.

Thank you to C.G. and A.P.;
Without you two, who would I be.
Thank you for the endless years,
All of the laughs and tears.
Thank you for the love and sisterhood you
have given freely over the last two decades.

Thank you to Elizabeth;
for your time, boost to my confidence when I doubted
this project, and the critical eye of a Virgo.

Thank you to B.G;
for pushing me to my limits and out of my comfort
zone. You have helped to elevate so many facets of my
life... I will always be indebted to you.

Prologue

There are times in life that we are faced with a choice that makes us decide what we are really willing to do.

How far are we really willing to go.
What is the extent we will we go to, to support ourselves and the ones that we love.

When we must face choices that others would shun you for, It is then that you find how deep the survival instinct runs within you.

I started my dancing era when I was 23. I didn't wake up one day and think that this was my dream job. It wasn't the choice I thought I would be making as a little girl. In fact, I had never imagined myself dancing for money. But life has a way of taking the reigns when you think you have control, and setting you on another course.

As such, I found myself dumped on a new path. There I was, newly divorced, I had a baby to take care of, two low paying jobs, and a new apartment I had to pay the rent on. Plus all the utilities, food, and basic life needs.

All by myself.

My new ex husband was not contributing to any of the costs towards raising our daughter, and day care was beyond expensive.

The options that I had were to either keep working 7-days a week, over a multitude of varying shifts, hoping I could find a sitter while waiting for the school list to open... or work a few nights a week making the same - if not more- money while getting to spend time with my baby.

There are a bevy of people who will look at my decision and say it was the wrong one. They will turn their nose up in judgement at me because the choice I made to take care of my child involved selling a little piece of me and, honestly, my soul.

Mind you, I was working. I had two jobs. This wasn't a case of I had no other option and took the easy way. It was, however, the best option to give me back time without shipping my daughter off to every aunt and grandparent.

Working the two jobs, I never had any time to spend with my daughter. Call me crazy, but I would rather spend time with my child if it means sacrificing a little bit of my wholesomeness.

And that is how I ended up with the stories you're about to read. So embark with me on a journey into just one of the many facets that exist in the underbelly of society.

Your friend does it for $50

I bent over, spreading my cheeks wide knowing the black thong would still prevent the guy behind me from seeing exactly what he wanted to see. I knew he was going to do what came next, his type always did. Sure enough, as I looked backwards he reached his hand forward, thinking he could manipulate the situation- my panties- to his liking. I took a step forward, turning to face him, a swift move of practice to avoid his hands groping and me having to shut him down. I wanted him to spend more money on me, so I had to play along for now.

I smiled at him, running my hands over my bare breasts, not letting him see the irritation at him thinking he could move my panties to the side. Not letting him know I knew what he was about to do.

I stepped in closer, swaying my near naked body to the beat of the music, my hands coming down to the arms of the chair. I got closer to him with my whole body, always moving so that no part of my body came into contact with his for to long.

He reacted exactly how I had hoped, moving his hands to the arm rests so I could sit on his lap.

"Bout time you see what I have here for you", he thrust his hips up as he said this, smiling at me.

We were deep in the game, both of us players in an age old competition. I giggled coquettishly, keeping my body lifted off his, still gyrating to the music,

"What did you bring me?", I teased.

He tried to lift his hand up to touch me again, and I deftly moved away. If you were good enough, the customers didn't realize you were trying to steer clear of their wandering hands and thought it was either part of the seduction or just ill timed.

This one was like a slippery eel, no matter how much I swayed and moved to and fro, he found some of my skin to touch. I loathed when they touched me and it was all I could do to not shirk away.

Finally I sat on him, leaning my back to his chest, with my head on his shoulder. I gyrated my hips, letting him feel the pressure of me sitting on him through his clothes. He tried to nuzzle my ear. I cringed at this move, my nose betraying what I was trying to hide as it wrinkled in disgust. It was to intimate, to personal.

"How about another dance?" I asked.

"Are you gonna give me what I want?" He replied.

I looked around the private dance room, not answering him. I had a moment until the song was over before I had to reply to him. The songs here were always short, that was the one good thing about this club, that and the short stage sets. The room was almost empty, with one other girl naked in the corner.

"And what is it you want?" I countered.

I knew what he wanted, and tried to not sigh out loud.

"A quick blowjob". And there it was

"No." I replied without pause.

"Your friend does it all the time" he countered.

"Does she?" I said, trying to mask my shock.

"Ya, and for only $50" he thought he snared me in.

"Hmm, I don't think I can" I said, finitely,

I stood up, shaking my ass, looking around the room and then sat back down. It gave me a moment to find composure and a reply.

"The room isn't empty and its to busy. Want another dance for $20?" I countered him.

"No. I'm all set." His tone was clear, he was done.

The song on the jukebox came to an end, pausing for half a beat before the next one came on. The music never stopped, but inside the private dance room the jukebox would take a break. I sat in the chair gathering my clothes from the floor in front of me.

I watched him go and sighed to myself. Reaching down to slide my shorts over my heals I saw something sticking out from under the chair.

I reached for it, it could be money, only to find an empty condom wrapper.

I held it for a moment. Disgust rolled through me, the last words he said replaying through my head.

"Your friend does it all the time".

See, sex is a business, and like any other business everyone is trying to save money or get the best deal. A customer will lie to get what they want; they'll try to barter with you, tell you someone else offered it cheaper, say everyone is doing it, whatever they have to do to save a buck or get something taboo, something they shouldn't have.

It wasn't the first time I heard those words, but for the first time I was contemplating if they were accurate.

The thing is, I had been out of the game for awhile. I came back to work with my girl to get some extra cash, as times were tight. We used to run the circuit together, traveling throughout the tri-state region going from club to club. But I had hung my thongs up months ago.

She hadn't.

I sat there for a moment, using the time to dress myself and gather my belongings as a farce to take in the room. It was small for a private dance area, with about 6 chairs lining the room and a jukebox guarding the door. There was one other girl in there with me, she had just walked in and was feeding the jukebox its one dollar fee to start the next song. She was holding her customer by his hand, he was eyeing her.

I sighed to myself, wrapping the money I had made in two rubber bands and sliding it into my little coin purse. I was counting the hours until this shift was over. I had to wait for the night to end before I could leave; I didn't drive and my girl was off making her money.

Dressed now, or as close to dressed as one could be working as a stripper, I made my way out of the corner leaving the condom wrapper, wishing my disgust would stay with it. I composed my face into the well known mask of a come hither smile, and sauntered out heading to the bar.

I didn't say anything to my friend. What I did do was start to pay attention to what she was doing. Up until then I had been working the room, trying to immerse myself back into the scene hoping to make as much money that night as I could so I didn't have to come back again.

"Where are you going?" I asked her as she zipped by me. "Just to the bathroom sweetie", she said, deftly sliding her arm away from my touch with eyes only for the door across the club. I turned my direction to follow her, as we hadn't really talked once we left the dressing room.

I didn't know anyone here aside from her, either customer or dancers and other staff while she seemed to be friends with everyone. As I chased her into the women's room I saw her go into the stall with another dancer, laughing. The bathroom had a few other girls in it, none of them my friend. The looked me up and down, knowing I was with her, but not knowing anything else, I was still an outsider. I checked my hair in the mirror, not adding to or paying attention to the conversation that was going on around me.

This was the public bathroom, with the music from the club pumping in over the speakers keeping the atmosphere still upbeat but masking any noise that could be overheard. As I checked my hair and makeup in the mirror, I strained to hear what was coming from the stall without looking like I was straining to hear anything from the stall.

Sighing, which seemed to be the theme of the night thus far, I gathered myself and walked out of the bathroom and back to the track.

Later that night we sat in the car outside the club. I was so tired, not having been up this late in quite some time. I was counting the final tally, after having paid out the club and the DJ, and walked with a crisp eight hundred thirty four dollars. I laughed, as there was a stack of ones that couldn't be folded.

She laughed next to me, "the stage did well for you like always. I hate the fucking stage."

I laughed, "this stack of ones doesn't add up to nearly as much as what you made in privates and back rooms."

That's how it had always been, I would rake in the money on the stage while she would prevail in getting private dances and champagne, or back, rooms.

"We just have to drop one of the other girls off real quick" she said.

My head snapped up, this was not part of the plan and I was so tired.

"She lives right off the road we take home, its the only reason I said we could do it, and it won't take long."

I stared at her. I was trying to not let my irritation show. "ok, that's fine." I said.

It was not fine, I thought.

We drove through the back roads home, veering off course right where she had told me we would. Here we go, I thought to myself. The speed we had been driving was abnormally slow, like that of someone who is trying to be extra careful, very aware, almost over compensating for something.

The girl in the back however, was rambling on about something to do with why she needed a ride and how mad she was. I tried to not listen, I was over this night already and just wanted to be home taking a shower.

We pulled into a driveway not to long thereafter, which made me happy. She wasn't lying about that part at least, which instantly made me question myself and why I thought that. She hadn't lied before, why did I insert that there? I'd have to come back to that thought once I was home, which shouldn't be to much longer.

"Let's go in real quick, I have to pee and I don't want to leave you in the car." She said as she turned the car off and opened her door.

I tried to not let her see my jaw hanging open as I sat in shock.

FUCK.

I sighed, again the theme of the evening, released my seat belt and opened the car door. I followed the two of them into the house, no idea of where I was going or whose house I was entering.

FUCK FUCK.

There is something off putting about walking into a lit up house at near 2:45 am, with two other girls having just gotten done selling yourselves all night, with the music going and the sound of men streaming out.

As we walked into the belly of the house, passing the mud room, we came into a living room with two white guys, video games, a dingy couch, some pipes with weed, and music playing. A classically stereotypical vision of what one would expect to come home to working in this field.

I felt out of place as the girl showed my friend down the hall and to the bathroom, and I awkwardly sat on an opposing chair from the guys. After a minute one of them spoke up "wanna hit this?", holding a pipe out with a lighter in his hand.

"No thanks" I smiled at him, "I'm already tired and that definitely wont help" I smiled wider, a yawn coming upon me at that very moment.

He looked at me, not smiling and not frowning, "Ok."

A few more moments passed as we sat there. I wasn't talking and neither were they. What was there to say after all. I think he was insulted that I didn't take his offer to smoke, but the truth was I didn't smoke out of pipes that weren't mine or my friends. I didn't know who these guys were and what they could have smoked out of it before they filled it with weed tonight.

My friend came out then, from down the hall with the girl she had given a ride home to. She did take the pipe from the guys, sparking the bowl and pulling a nice long drag in. She blew out a thick smoke cloud, handing the bowl back. I zoned out while the four of them seemed to finish the bitching the girl had been doing in the car. It was something about why her boyfriend, bowl offerer, couldn't come get her.

I didn't care, but I seemed to be the only one. My friend finally noticed and asked if I was ready to head out, which was only a pleasantry as it was apparent from the resting bitch face I was unable to hide. When we got back in the car she was acting overly cautious again while driving, something that was very unusual.

Sitting in the dark I replayed the night. As scenes and sounds whirled past the movie screen behind my eyes, I realized I was headed in one direction. Try as I might, the thought latched on and I couldn't dislodge it. "Are you doing coke?" I blurted it out.

FUCK.

"What?! NO?!" She defended herself.

"You can tell me. I would rather know and you be honest with me about it than have to guess or wonder."

"Of course not. Why would you think that? I just didn't know where the bathroom was and she had to show me. Then earlier tonight the girl in the bathroom asked for my help with an outfit."

"What about you doing a dance and running off to the bathroom. You did a bunch of dances but you said you didn't make money tonight. You were in the bathroom for a long time and it seemed like you had been in the house before. You are driving funny and you seem to have the sniffles. Maybe you aren't, but something is off about you tonight. At least to me. You never used to want to stop anywhere, let alone hang out for 20 minutes because thats how long we were in there for. You are just a whole different person from who I used to work with."

She didn't say anything as we drove the rest of the way to the park and ride I had met her at earlier.

It was a long ride.

That was the last night that I worked as a stripper.

The Beginning

I still remember the very first night I worked at a strip club. I went in during the day and asked to speak to someone about working there. They took one look at me, a young girl at the ripe old age of 23, and told me to come back that night for 6pm. Nothing else - no audition, no take off your clothes, they didn't even ask if I had danced before. Looking back, they likely new I was fresh meat. I reeked of it.

I went home and gathered what I thought would be an okay outfit
-1 pair of thongs
-1 pair of cheeky underwear
-1 bra
-1 belly shirt
-a pair of low heels

I threw all this into a backpack with some makeup, and made my way to the club for 6pm.

When I got there I was shown up to the dressing room by one of the guys who worked there. He grabbed one of the other girls and told her to give the new girl some pointers. She looked me up and down, and told me to let her know when I was ready. I sat there nervously, hoping I didn't look as startled as I felt. I had no idea what I was doing.

"Walk the club, try to get dances, show up to your stage set. Guys will try to get free anything from you, don't fall for it. The real money is in the champagne rooms, hopefully you get one of those, that would be great for your first night. I had one a few weeks back, the guy just wanted me to sit and talk to him. He ended up keeping me back there..." I was trying to listen, but as we walked around the club my thoughts took off.

I laughed at her, she said something funny and it was perfectly timed. It seemed to satisfy her, and she said "ok, that's the club! Good luck and make lots of money. Just remember, ask them for dances". And just like that, she was flouncing off and I stood there in my makeshift outfit with my subpar heels.

I had a little bit to catch my thoughts, as the club was empty. The other girls were settling into their nightly routine, ordering drinks or food and preparing for a night of entertaining men. I took this all in; the women who had been doing this for longer than I had thought about it.

It was obvious that I was the new girl on the block, not only from my outfit but even my demeanor. There is a certain attitude that develops when you spend a lot of time walking around a public place with little to no clothes on, vying for money based on your appearance. It's hard to put your finger on just what it is that separates the two worlds. A mixture of confidence, a hardness, and an air of not caring all collide to differentiate the shy new girl from the rest of the crowd.

I made money that night simply because men like to be the first for anything. It didn't matter what I looked like or how well - or bad- I danced. They could smell the innocence like a wolf catching the scent of its prey after an unintentional fast.

Bikini Bars

There was this bar in the city of Providence that would have women parade around in a top and a bottom, a 'bikini', dance on stage, and allow private dances down below in the basement. While in the bar they could not take off or show anything under the outfit. The bikini was never really just a bikini, as it was designed to be removed down below, in the creepiest of rooms ever encountered.

I went there the first night to visit My friend. She had started working there the week before and was making good money at what she said was called a bikini bar. When we walked in, me and another friend, I was a little surprised to find a narrow dimly lit bar, with room for no more than four seats. We sat here, unsure of where the rest of the place went and not brave enough to explore it just yet. Drinks were ordered, ridiculously overpriced as usual. It didn't seem like a bad place I thought, like any other bar. I swiveled in my chair to look behind me, and noticed there were a few girls walking around with a couple sitting amongst the row of the oversized chairs that ran along the walkway to the back, where a stage was located. The girls were in bright outfits that were not bikinis. Oh my, I thought, We are not in Kansas anymore. The outfits were bright colors, with fishnets, booty shorts, body suits made of fishnets, and all sorts of revealing outfits.

It's in times like this where you realize you just learned something you didn't know you didn't know. Bikini bars were not bars that girls just walked around in bikinis, and there was a whole market to this clothing thing that extended out of the strip clubs and into anything that was adult use.

As we sat there observing my friend walked over to us in her own skimpy outfit. "Hey!, you made it!". She was excited for me to be there, she wanted me to like it so I would come to work with her as she didn't want to keep doing it alone. She would she had said, but it would be nice to not have to do it alone.

"Come walk around with me", she said. Dragging me by the arm away from the bar and into the bellows of the beast. She giggled as we set off, her heels clacking on the floor with each step that she took. My footsteps were silent, despite the little heels I had worn.

As we walked deep into the bar she started pointing out parts that my eyes hadn't registered when I first walked in. Interesting I thought to myself, how the lights in the front are so bright it makes it hard to see in the back. There was a row of deep plush leather chairs off to one side of the wall, with another set of chairs facing the opposite direction just down the hall further. We reached the first stage, which was a pole placed on a rectangular platform, currently empty.

At the back of the bar we reached another bar, this one without bright lights and a half clad bartender in a bikini working. The room opened up a bit, making the whole place take on the shape of an 'I', with a bar serving drinks at each end.

I noticed a second stage tucked in the corner along with a wide staircase that descended to who knows where across from it. On the other end was a door that led outside.

Another girl in a bright pink fishnet bodysuit sauntered over holding the hand of a guy, and climbed on top of the barstool, sticking her rear into the air.

"Hiya can I get a vodka sprite", she said to the bartender, wiggling her butt as she looked back over towards the guy. "You buyin my drink, babe?" She asked him. Leaning into his side, wiggling a little slower. He fumbled into his pocket, pulling his wallet out. "Fifteen" the bartender said.

I stood in shock, watching how he would react to such a ridiculous priced drink. To my surprise he didn't balk at the price, but handed her a twenty and didn't resist as the pink fishnet girl sipped her drink pulling him away from the bar, leaving his change as a tip.

I was even more shocked when I watched her pull him to the stairs heading into what seemed like it could be a dungeon. "Where are they going?!" I turned to my friend and asked her in shock.

"Private dances are downstairs" she said. "Wanna go look?"

Bikini Bars to Strip Clubs

We worked in the downtown bikini bar for only another month. The more time we spent inside and around the customers the more we realized this was one of the old style clubs. The kind that we didn't want any part of. Although it seemed less risqué on the outward appearance, the secret dungeon-esque private rooms downstairs told another story.

"How about we check out one of the Mass clubs?" My friend asked me one day. "I know they're full nude, but at least its all up front instead of the tricks these nasty gashes are turning downstairs. I stopped making money as soon as the customers realized I wasn't selling the same menu"

"Shit I am down. I haven't ever made good money here. You can at least fake it until you get downstairs. I can't even lie my way into a dance." That was the truth. I couldn't lie to make money. I didn't have the skill set to sell something that wasn't really for sale, and the men could tell I wasn't about to give them what they were there for.

"Alright, lets get the fuck outta here then. I'm not making any money and I'm sick of walking this shit hole. I'm not paying them their house fee either so lets grab our shit and sneak out the back. We won't be back so fuck it if they ban us."

We headed back to the dressing room and began changing out of the slutty clothes and into the sweatpants that felt like heaven. I counted the dismal ones I had made that night. I wasn't paying the house shit with this payout. I didn't even break a hundred dollars. Sighing, I swung my bag on my shoulder and made my way to sneak out the back. I couldn't wait to leave this place behind.

I didn't make eye contact with anyone as we crept out of the dressing room and across the floor to the back door. There would be a few girls outside smoking, guaranteed. We opened the door and made our way down the fire exit steel stairs, walking past the two girls smoking. "They're gonna be pissed if you leave early", said the one in the long leopard print coat.

"Eh fuck it. We aren't coming back anyways!" My friend laughed, "have fun fucking and sucking".

I gasped, but she kept going

"You can't make shit in here if you aren't a prostitute".

I just got into the car and wished she would hurry. Tonight was not the night I wanted to get into a fight.

"Fucking dirty bitches, every one of them", she was still ranting as we sped off. "Can't make shit. Didn't make shit. And I'm hungry. We're finding a new club tomorrow."

And like that, we were done with the dingy secret brothel.

Secrets

The thing about a secret is that it is almost impossible for it to stay that way. No matter how hard you try, all it takes is a slip of a tongue or in this case a sighting with someone's eyes.

We thought we were working far enough away from home that people back home wouldn't find out. It's one thing to dance on a stage, and another to do it FOR people that you know and never wanted them to see you naked. The goal was to never have to face that mortifying moment you may have seen in the movies; The girl walks onstage and as she turns around naked, there is someone she knows. Depending on the person she either keeps going or runs off stage in a fit of tears.

The fit of tears would be regulated to family, the show would go on for anyone else that the dancer happened to know.

Naturally, the first night we started working at this new club we had our moment. We had gotten the club to start us on the stage together, which usually they would accommodate. We timed getting ready with our first stage set, so we didn't walk the club before we went on. That proved to be a mistake on our parts, especially with how close we were working to home.

The stage was in the shape of an 'L', with the entrance being the top of the letter. We had been on stage for only a little while when I noticed them, sitting down at the bottom of the L shaped stage.

I made my way over to my friend rather quickly when I realized that the two guys on the end were people that we knew.

"Fuck. Do you see who is over at the end of the stage. We know them." I hissed at her.

"Just dance like you don't know them" she hissed back.

I sighed to myself, careful to not let any of this interaction be seen from the customers point of view.

At some point we would have to make our way to that end of the stage. They had money put out and we couldn't just not take it. This was a quick range of emotions felt in a space that I could not truly express them. The nerves, embarrassment, and unease were bubbling right below the surface but there wasn't anything that I could do apart from keep dancing.

And that is what I did.

Even when I made my way over to the two guys sitting with money out on the stage that I happened to know.

I took their money, but I gave them a show that would either require them to put more up if they wanted any other interest. I acted as if I did not know them the entire time, and to my surprise they did not say anything to me.

I wasn't sure if they said anything to my friend, I would ask her after. I had a feeling that these two would not be keeping our secret to themselves, which I couldn't blame them. I knew I would do the same thing if I were in their shoes.

Later that night when we were getting changed in the dressing room, I asked her how the first stage set had went and whether or not they said anything to her. They had left shortly after we were on the stage, so it alleviated me from having to small talk with them on the floor.

"They didn't say much, they were kind of smirking the whole time like fucking assholes. They're probably going to run back to town and talk about it at the bar later on." She told me.

"I wouldn't be surprised if they did. I mean, I would" I told her.

And the truth was, if I saw someone I knew dancing, I would definitely be talking about it with someone. The level of hypocrisy in that was astronomically high, but it made for good banter about what was happening in a small town.

I knew that sooner or later word would get out that we were dancing at the local club and then it would spread to every one who gossiped like us.

Secrets can only be kept for so long.

Let's hit the road

After the little debacle at the local club, we had decided that we would never work close to home again. That was the one thing both of us had agreed upon when talking about schedules, to stay as far away as possible from the two local clubs. We had each danced a night at one of the two, alone and then together; after running into a friend of a friend of a friend, which is bound to happen in a small town, we stepped back and decided to travel.

The thing about this is that even leaving our local area we still weren't to far away from home. We weren't able to travel like some of the girls we worked with, that were actually flying to other states to dance there. We were young, dumb, and in need of money. And we had kids to raise which most of the traveling girls didn't have.

So we drove about an hour to an hour and a half away for. Neither one of us wanted to make the commute by ourselves, so during the week we would pick our nights together and this way we could drive up together. We had to be on stage for our first set at roughly 6-7pm, so we tried to head out of town around 4-5pm. This gave us enough time to drive there, grab some food on the way, and then get to the club and get ready.

Once the nerves went away, the drive to the club was a great time. We hyped ourselves up, playing music, smoking weed and having a great time with each other. I never drove, my car was older and it was never an option that was even mentioned.

My friend had a brand new Honda Accord, which was like comparing a burlap bag to silk, when it came to my car. What I could do, was roll blunts. I always sat down in the car and immediately started to roll up. We would smoke two blunts minimum on the ride there.

I was the only one who could roll up, so it was already my designated job when we would hang out. I would have both blunts rolled by the time we left the gas station, which timed with being on the outskirts of the town center. It was clear to light up once we passed out of the congested area.

We would smoke one blunt, listen to Lil' Wayne or some other billboard hit, and almost always stop to grab some type of dinner. Depending on which club we were working at, we would usually have a few designated options that we had come to enjoy.

One of my favorite places was this little pizza shop that we had accidentally ended up at one day. It was in a strip mall, off a random high way exit that wasn't quite near anything in particular.

We would order a small cheese pizza with French fries and split it. The pizza was always fresh and made with the perfect sauce and a crust with just enough crunch. It was a mom and pop pizza place, with a bunch of young cute guys working the ovens. It was a delight on all the senses when we grabbed pizza.

Other times we would stop at chain restaurants and grab a burger or a grinder. We usually ate once on the way, which saved a little bit of money over the food at the club. Plus we didn't like to eat while we were making money, so dinner in the car on the way in to work was usually the order of operations.

Once we were done with dinner, we would light the second blunt up. This would take us right to the parking lot of the club. We finished the blunt in the car, with smoke billowing out of the windows. For some reason this always garnered more attention than if we were drinking in the car. But no matter how much they disliked the smell of weed, we always showed up smoked out.

Auditions

The one thing I didn't plan on was having to audition. We showed up at a club my friend had read about in a magazine she found at an adult toy store. "Can we talk to someone about working here?" The security guy looked us over now that we declared ourselves as not customers. "Sure hold on".

He walked over to his podium and grabbed a walkie-talkie that was tucked underneath. "I got two girls who wanna work".

"Send them back"

"Alright, you're gonna head straight to the bar, go around it and at the back is a door. Go knock on it".

We headed to the back of the bar, following around it like instructed. It was dark, the music was loud and I tried to take in the layout of the place while we walked through the club. One stage, one mini stage, each with a pole. Chairs all around the stage, with a huge bar. I could see food being brought out as we rounded the corner to head towards the back of the club. I was starving, but we decided to wait to eat. Smelling the chicken wings didn't help the nerves in my stomach any.

Here we go I thought, as my friend knocked on the door. 'Yeah!" I heard, muffled through the door. We opened it and walked in to a much quieter space. Once the door was shut you could actually hear people talking. What I saw was exactly what I expected. A large man sitting behind a desk. The only thing missing was the pile of money and cocaine; maybe it was just to early. "So you wanna dance in my club, let me see what you look like. Go change into an outfit and come back." Bathroom is out this office and to the right."

We walked back out and made our way to the bathroom, which was the next door down across the hall. 'Fuck, what are we gonna do- I didn't bring anything to wear." "panties and bras" Strip down, and lets head back.

"Fuck, fuck - I didn't wear anything that matches". I sighed to myself. I was not put together enough for this. I hadn't expected to have to audition, although it made sense. I stripped the clothes off, folded them, and carried them back with us, our bundles tucked underneath each of our arms. We stepped out of the bathroom and I felt so exposed, so not ready to walk back into this office in my mis-matched bra and panty 'outfit'.

"Nope, I don't do tattoos". We hadn't even done a full circle around and he had already said no! What the fuck was this?! "But there's a girl out there with tattoos right now!" We countered.

"She's been here. I'm not taking on more. Thanks for coming out."

With that, we traipsed back to the bathroom and got dressed. Well, that was an interesting experience. "I bet it was my mismatched panties" I said.

She laughed. "Good, this place isn't even that busy, there's another place we can try. Let's head there."

"Can we grab some food first. Rejection still sucks."

We walked back through the club, with a few of the customers looking us over as we walked out. The security guard knew the decision already, because as we walked by he told us to have a good night and "come back in a few months, the girls are always changing in here".

I smiled at him 'thanks have a great night", and walked through the door back outside. I sighed. I couldn't help but feel that being unprepared was the cause of his no. We didn't even get all the way in front of him before he said no, and the tattoos we each had we so tiny there was no way it could have been for them.

"This sucks."

I didn't know how to take this; it was one thing to be passed up because you weren't a prostitute, another because the manager didn't like how you looked. "ok, so this is a lesson I guess, we need to be prepared for the next club. Our tattoos aren't shit compared to that tweaker looking bitch that was on the stage. I don't like being rejected at a damn audition."

Let's Get out of This Town

We drove out to Springfield Massachusetts to this club that I had never heard of. I'm not sure where she had heard of it either, but there we were, standing in front of the house mom.

"Okay, you're going to work here tonight. You'll be on the same stage set, each set is 30 minutes and there are 4 sets. You will be grouped with other girls too. Tonight you go on once every 2 hours, if there are more girls you go less and less girls you go more. Tonight we'll see how you do up on the stage and then we'll talk about where and when you can work. You have 1 hour to get ready, I want you on the stage for 7pm sharp. The dressing room is behind me. Find a spot that isn't taken and use it. We have cameras in here, so don't worry about anyone fucking with your stuff. On the nights you do work, we have beds you can rent on the third floor so you don't have to drive home. We have girls that come here from all over to work the weekends. The DJ has your stage names, he will give a little intro as you hop up on stage. Let me know if you have any questions and good luck."

She popped her gum and was off, talking in her walkie-talkie :"we've got two new ones on set 2." her voice trailed off as we walked away and into the dressing room.

This place was unlike any other spot we had been in. This wasn't a dingy basement, or a cramped closet for a dressing room. This was the second floor of an old mill and it was amazing. There were rows of mirrors with lights, the first thought that came to mind was this must be what a dressing room of Vegas show girls must be like.

There were comfortable chairs and outlets to plug your hair tools into. There were several cameras around, and that made me feel good. It sucks to be watched, but when you're leaving your stuff in a bag inside a dressing room you become thankful for it; most of the girls we encountered were not the type that you would trust.

We dropped our stuff on two empty tables and started pulling out the bevy of clothes, makeup, and styling tools that went into putting the new personality on. That's what it was for me. When I was sitting in the chair, I was painting the makeup on over the proper, demure girl and allowing the seductive saleswoman to come out. Make no mistake, stripping is not just about taking your clothes off and looking good. You are selling an idea, a fantasy, to the men that didn't always want it. It's easy for them to drop a few dollar bills on a stage, but convincing them to spend twenty dollars on a private dance was no easy feat.

I was so nervous, painting the persona on. I never wore quite as much makeup as everyone else, I was never that good at it. I did the basics, but the contouring and art work that others did was beyond me. I watched the other girls getting ready to see how they put their makeup on, learning new color combinations and techniques.

We toyed through our outfits, I had a couple different things I had picked up at the local adult store in between our failed audition and tonight's adventure. I hadn't made to much money yet, so I didn't invest heavily into my outfits. I had gone and bought a proper pair of stripper heels though, and now that I had those I felt like I belonged.

I decided I was going to keep my outfit basic at three small pieces plus shoes - basically a bikini plus thongs. I hated my boobs, because I didn't have any. I did have an ass though, it was all natural and made up for the lack of a chest. There is a song that talks about a large bottom and up top being the equivalent of an insect bite. I'm not that bad, but pretty close. The new platform heels were the finishing touch, and they gave me the confidence boost to feel like I might actually belong.

We were ready, and it was almost 7pm. I gave one last look in the mirror, sighed deeply, and looked at my friend. "Let's do this". She smiled at me, "we're gonna make money tonight! Look at this place!"

With that, we zipped our stuff up and placed it on the seat. "Ok, lets go".

The walk down into the club was horrible. My stomach twisted into knots as I walked down the stairs, hoping nobody could actually see my legs shaking. These shoes were easy to walk in, but I felt disconnected from the ground and I wasn't exactly ready to be descending a grand staircase like I was Scarlet fucking O'Hara.

I gripped the railing tight and slowly put one foot in front of the other, looking at where my feet were going. I knew I looked like a baby giraffe trying to walk for the first time, but honestly I would rather look that way than be bouncing down the stairs. Then I would never be able to show my face again, let alone work here.

I reached the bottom and let out a sigh of relief. I took my hand off the railing and flexed it, releasing the tension that was there from holding on so tight. My hand was clammy too, great.

"Jesus" I muttered under my breath.

"No shit", my friend said. "what a fucking entrance".

I laughed and it seemed like we both inhaled and exhaled together. "ok, now that that's done, lets see what we're working with."

We set off together, leaving the staircase behind and descended into the belly of the club. The staircase was near the entrance, so new comers and dancers would enter at the same place in a smaller room that abutted the larger room containing the bar. This antechamber was a spillover for really busy nights. It had a small round stage with a pole, as well as tables and chairs for people to sit. It was currently empty, and so we continued on into the main part.

We entered the room, and immediately stopped.

"Holy shit."

"Holy shit is right."

The bar was the stage. The stage was the bar. We both stood there, right as the clock struck 7 and the DJ came over the speaker.

"Aaand that wraps up those sexy ladies, all will be available for private dances or a private room upstairs!

Next we have a real treat, a devilish duo of two new girls both on the stage for your enjoyment. Show Mallory and Bree some love..and here they are now."

Our legs had gotten the message as he started talking and we had moved over to where the other girls were climbing off the stage. Where the bar would normally open to let the bar staff go behind it was a short ladder that we used to climb up as he was announcing us.

Please don't fucking fall, I thought to myself. My arms and legs were shaking as I stood up and looked down at all the men sitting around the bar staring at me. I stopped at the first dollar bill that was resting on the stage and started to gyrate my hips and move my body.

It was only one dollar, but as soon as I started to dance he and his friend put out more money. I opened my top, sliding the two covers over to the side so that my nipples were now out. More money was put on the stage. As I was dancing I looked around me, and realized the stage was huge and there was a lot of money to be made. I grabbed the money I had made so far, smiled at the two guys and told them I would be back with a wink. "I'll be back, I don't want to keep you all to myself."

I was already on my hands and knees, so I simply crawled over to the next couple of guys. "Hey you, hows your night going?" I asked, as I wiggled my hips back and forth making my ass jiggle.

"Well helllo there, you're one of the new girls aren't you?"

"I am!, its my first night".

"Like first night dancing, or first night here?"

I fibbed a little and replied "first night dancing, I'm so nervous, I'm here with my friend."

"you're going to do great tonight, with a body like that don't even worry" His friend looked at him, 'why don't you take her for her first dance once she's done, I'll even pay for it".

"Ok, when you're done on stage come see me".

"I will!" I replied "I'm gonna keep moving around the stage but I'll be back" and smiled as I moved around the stage.

I made it around the stage completely once before I saw her again, she came up to me in the center which was as far away from the customers as we could get.

"I hate this stage, I feel like I'm going to fall off if I step in the wrong spot" she said.

"I almost did!" I said to her.

The stage was set up so the bartenders could get to all the customers, and so could the dancers, so it had a walkway that was like a moat around the center of the stage. We had to cross the moat to get to the customers, which meant that one wrong step and 'Dancer Down' was all that I could think of.

"I hate how long we have to be up here, but I like that we aren't alone" She said.

"It's not so bad with a bunch of us up here. Have you done okay so far?" I was looking at the bills I had made so far on the stage, pleased with the outcome.

The Other Girls

There is an expression, that you think everyone has common sense until you work in retail. I'm not sure if there is one for girls who work in strip clubs, although I'm betting its got a jab at their daddy issues.

I didn't take much time to talk to the other girls, everyone was hustling and I had my friend with me for camaraderie. Sometimes, depending on the club we were working at there might have been a friendly face that one of us would talk to. We were up to working at three to four clubs on the regular depending on where we got put that week.

We met Ashlee at the BeeGee2 backstage on the first night we were scheduled to work. She was tall, ebony and beautiful, a triple threat in a backwoods area. We had walked in that first night, and she had her right foot placed on top of the counter, her head bent over looking at herself as she wiped away whatever she was looking for. She looked up at us, her eyes traveling over the two of us standing there, her legs open, and asked if we hit a skunk on the way in, without a care in the world.

"Hiya, I'm Ashlee" she said, standing up and adjusting her bikini bottoms back to normal. "This must be your first night, I haven't seen you yet." It wasn't a question.

"ya, first night"I said, as we walked in to the dressing room. We zeroed in on an empty space on the counter, carefully claiming a little bit of space and an electrical outlet.

We were waiting for the DJ to come in to let us know when we would be on stage while we set up our makeup and pawed through our bags. I cautiously looked around the room, not wanting to make eye contact with anyone or let them see me staring at them. Just because it is a bunch of women in the back doesn't mean it's always a friendly environment. In fact it is quite the opposite, as everyone around you is vying for the same money. There were no friends, just competition.

But I am a curious person and like to study people, so while pulling my face powders and eye colors out, I stole glances at everyone who was around me. What were they wearing, how were they doing there makeup. Nobody wants to be someone's twin on accident, let alone if they don't know or like them.

As I studied the women around me I took in their appearances. Short. Tall. Shorter. Big boobs. BIG boobs. Super fake boobs. No boobs. Dark. Light. Asian. Ghetto. Bougee. Fake lips. Fake everything.

"Bree and Mallory!" Bellowed the DJ as he came barreling through the side door in the dressing room. I snapped out of my observation and looked at him, "yeah!" I said in tandem with my friend.

"You two are up on the quarter hour. I'll put you together tonight but don't expect it every time even if you ride in together." He said, as his eyes roved over the dressing room

"Hey Sam, lookin good tonight" he said to the short girl on the end.

"Shut the fuck up Billy", Sam said through pouted lips as she applied her red lipstick.

Billy the DJ laughed and went back through the door he had just come in through. I looked at the clock and noted I had forty five minutes to get ready.

Sam spoke up as soon as the door shut. "I hate that fucking prick. He just walks in here like its not a women's dressing room." She sighed, and threw her lipstick down. Turned around and bent over to pull her thigh high tights up over her skinny legs.

The more I looked at her, I realized how little she really was. She had on ridiculously high stripper heels and still was only about five feet tall. She had long black hair, and pale ivory skin. She threw her hair over her shoulder as she headed for the door. I watched her walk out and set back to my task at hand.

Ashlee spoke up next, "don't listen to her. She loves when he comes in here. All she does is tell stories." I glanced at her in the mirror, smiling a little at the friendliness of any type of conversation. Ashlee bopped around the room, getting ready.

"Ya'll new here. It's not so bad, you'll make some money tonight. There's not to many girls and its been getting busier on Sundays. I work all up and down the coast, and I like it here. I just came up from Florida and WHAAAT it is wild down there, let me tell you. Mmhmm, good money."

I was intrigued, and started listening.

Natalee was tall and skinny with long blonde hair and a nose that reminded me of Paris Hilton. She was up on the stage and I was making the usual circuit around the BeeGee Two on a slow Sunday night. The path all the girls walked around the oval stage was the same, and we walked it so much that it was surprising there wasn't a path worn out in the floor. Round and round the stage I thought to myself.

It was early in the night but it was slower than usual and I didn't have much hope for the night to improve. I sighed, thinking about how I owed the house and the DJ and had to get a few dances. I looked around and saw one guy at the stage. Natalee was twirling around in her skimpy shiny reflective metallic bikini, trying to gain the sole wallets attention.

Round and round we go.

I glanced at the private dance section as I rounded the tale end of the oval, opposite where Natalee was. There were a couple of girls occupied but I didn't see any guys that were free and looking for conversation or a dance.

Rounding the bottom of oval I noticed that Natalee had gotten his attention. Hmmm, interesting I thought. The thing about Natalee is that she had no boobs, and no hips. When I say no, I don't mean little... I mean twelve year old boy with just nipples no boobs and no hips. She was unattractive at all, but she was not the typical body type that you would expect to see in a strip club. Call me a stereotyper, but tits and ass are the two things that patrons look for, followed by face and favors.

By the time I got to the top of the oval Natalee was laying on her side on the stage, one leg in the air with her back towards me. Her customer was staring at her intently, his eyes transfixed on her. I round the stage, Natalee on my right side, and then I saw what the interest was. She had her panties pulled to the side, and was playing with herself very discreetly on stage. The state we were in was a bottoms-on state with alcohol, which means no kitty cat on display.

Faces and favors. Natalee was playing with herself on stage in a bottoms only club and he was paying her very well while she was up there. She looked at me as I looked at her. I realized how she made her money then, and she looked at me with a challenge to judge her. It wasn't her I was judging though, it was all the customers that went to her.

The Customers

BeeGees was crowded and I was walking around the bar and stage combo. There were a lot of girls on tonight, a mix of all sorts of flavors. I was hoping to make good money, but knew it was going to be competitive. I kept meeting intersecting with a new girl at the top of the circular track we were both walking, smiling as we looped around again. She was really pretty with caramel skin tone and dark, curly hair that was at her chin.

I noticed that we both kept eyeing this younger Latino kid, maybe just turned twenty one I thought dismally, but cute. See, there are different types of customers, and usually the younger good looking guys wouldn't spend money. They may tip girls at the bar, or buy them a drink but it was rare that they would drop money on private dances and champagne rooms without a special occasion. My friend didn't talk to them because in her eyes they wouldn't spend enough money as easily as an older guy.

But he was cute. I liked cute boys. Especially the ones that looked like they got into trouble on the streets making poor life decisions. Naturally I sauntered up to him to strike up a conversation.

"Hiii, hows your night?" I coyly said to him, a smile on my lips.

He licked his lips before he replied "its good. I've been watching you, you're beautiful. My name is Louis."

"Mallory" I replied. "I'm new here, its my first real night working. Last week was the audition. It was so nerve wracking" I laughed.

The song changed and the DJ came over the loudspeaker. "And that's the end of these beautiful girls on stage, next up we have another group of gorgeous women ready to tantalize and tease you here at the BeeGee"

"Shit, that's me." I said to Louis.

"I'll see you up there" Louis said, a slow sly smile coming across his face.

I grinned back at him and turned to walk away, making my way over to the ladder that would lead me up to the bar top. It happened to be across the room. Of course I thought to myself. My biggest fear, still, was walking in front of people. All I could think of was falling. What if my shoe slipped on a wet spot from someone's spilled drink, or I lost my footing on a step. To avoid this, I just walked slowly. I sauntered to the stage, keeping an eye on where I placed each step.

I climbed up the ladder, sliding my hands up and making sure I placed the ball of each foot on a rung. The ladder was only three rungs up, but again, I did not want to fall and that included through the ladder. Taking a deep breathe I switched into the stage mode.

Confident.

Sexy.

Slutty.

My eyes found their sultry come hither lenses as I used the top of the ladder like it was a gymnasts horse, tucking my knees up and swinging back and forth until I stomped my heels down on the top of the stage. I stood up to my full height and honed in on the closest man, which was directly in front of me. I began the slow slither that he expected for the ones he had placed in front of him. I scooped them in my hand, waiting to see if he would place more.

If he put more up while I was in front of him then the expectation was for me to keep going. If I took the money and he didn't place more then I would move away an onto the next guy. At least that's what my rules were. Sometimes when I would go to leave then they would place more money and I would stay.

This was like a game of chicken, which one of us will cave first. The girl trying to earn her money for as little skin as possible, or the customer wanting to see as much as possible for as cheap as possible. The winner could be determined by the age old decider in business: supply and demand.

If a customer found themselves inside on a slow night then they are going to get a lot more attention than on a busy night with money flowing freely from all directions.

I had a goal this night though, and that was making my way around the stage over to Louis. It wasn't often that we would get cute young guys who also spent money. At least not for me, and not in this club.

See, there were different types of customers.

If they were young, cute and they know it means they will spend <u>minimal</u> money on the girls, but definitely on the liquor. They will buy you a drink, but "don't need to pay for pussy."

But, if they were young, nerdy, and maybe got picked on in school then this means they will like one or two specific girls and will spend money on them, but definitely not the mean girls.

Bachelor parties are a mixed lot. Younger guys who want to spend money, older guys who have been there done that and usually always a first timer in the mix. They always go for the hard core stripper of the club who can pick up dollars with their ass cheeks.

That leaves the old men, who will always spend money on the girls, including buying them food. They're usually picky about a type, but love the new girls. Dirty old men is a real thing. I will never look at grandpas the same.

Louis was not old, he was not dorky, and he seemed like he may spend a little bit of money. That was the trade off sometimes; less money with someone you can tolerate rather than more money from someone who you just didn't want to dance for. But it was more than that. He was nice, with nice eyes and a nice smile.

Selling sex shows you the side of people that is hidden from most of polite society. Nobody expects grandpa with the white beard pulling off the Kris Kringle look to talk about the smell of your vagina, or the old man who has a cane to ask you to sit on his lap and help him ejaculate.

Meeting someone in the same setting that is the exact opposite can be a breathe of fresh air. And that's what Louis was. And he smelled good. I was able to bypass all the filled seats and find Louis. He was at the end, sitting there with a drink and no money in front of him. He saw me, and as I got closer he put out a five. I smiled as I tried to slow my walk over to him.

I skipped right to floor work and squatted down, bending backwards so that my left hand was behind me on the floor and I was looking down my stomach at Louis. My knees were splayed wide, my heels giving me an extra bit of height as I leaned back. I smiled at him and ran my right hand down my throat and chest, over my legs.

As the song wore on, I kept dancing and Louis kept putting money up. I crawled across the stage, balancing on the bar top careful to keep his drink where it belonged and not on the floor from an errant foot. As I moved in front of him, he smiled at me.

"I love the way you dance for me".

He sat back, his drink in his hand and enjoyed every moment I spent enjoying him. There really is something to different about dancing for someone who excites you versus dancing for someone who is just paying you. Don't get me wrong, Louis was paying me, we were both there for a reason, but it just wasn't the same as the dirty old men who are out trying to cheat on their wife.

Louis came and visited me every week for as long as I worked at the BeeGee. He never once bought a private dance, but he spent the same amount of money while at the stage. He would always wait until I went up on the stage, smiling as he caught my eye. I would never make him wait for me, always going to him as soon as I noticed he was there.

I can still see his young face in my memories, hear those words in my head.

"I love the way you dance for me."

I think about what may have happened to Louis all the time. I knew what he was as soon as we started talking. There are some things that only fit in with someone who deals with the dark world of mind altering substances, and that was everything that Louis was. Even now certain songs will play on the radio and that sweet handsome smile pops into my head with those eight words.

"I love the way you dance for me."

Slow Nights

Everyone thinks that every night of working in a strip club is going to be raking in the dough. But that is not the case. There are some nights that the club puts so many girls on the schedule that you are competing with four other girls that look just like you.

The stage sets are changed. Instead of thirty minutes, they reduce it to twenty. Instead of one or two girls it becomes three of four girls.

Those nights you better be hustling. In some cases its not just about how someone looks and whether or not the men like their body. It's how good of a salesman they are, and do the people there want to buy. Other nights its as simple as you are someone's type, or they picked you out of all the girls walking around.

To make money on a night with a lot of girls you have to be ON. Selling personality, paradise and false promises. Conversations have to be started, a decision formed, and action taken all within a few moments. If it is decided there is no money to be made then it is on to the next person.

The opposite can also happen, where there are no customers who come in! Even if there are a small number of girls if there is no money coming in the door then there is no money to be made. The poor guys who do come in get pounced on like they are carrying the first drop of water that has been seen after getting lost in the Sahara for a week.

Going home with no money is the worst feeling ever. And it happens.

In fact, sometimes not only is no money made, but after paying the house fee dancers leave with less money than when they started the night. The nights that the club sat empty were not as minimal as everyone would think. On those nights, how can money be made when there is no money coming through the door?

It can't.

Couple the lack of customers with an over abundance of girls working, and when someone does walk in, its like a frenzy of piranhas as everyone tries to claim their stake.

In an industry that is composed of reactions to physical appearance, going home with no money can be the biggest detriment to ones self confidence and feeling of self worth. Sitting at home in the wee hours of the morning, after a night of traipsing around a club in next to nothing, selling fantasies, with no money to show for leaves an empty feeling inside.

For an industry that is made up of women who notoriously have "daddy issues", its not hard to see how this feeling of lack of self worth can only help said daddy issues. It is a cycle that is created, ups and downs of feeling good followed by feeling low. Where a high paying night often leaves people feeling amazing, and a low paying night leaves them feeling as if they aren't worthy of anyone. It's a bitch to have your body connected to validation.

But on a good night, its the exact opposite. Sitting in the dressing room after killing it all night. Your feet are aching, your knees are sore from the stage, but in your hand is a stack of twenties and hundreds. In that moment, its as if you are Queen Cleopatra and you are walking slowly down the carpet in your palace to the men that are bowed, begging to kiss the ground you walk on.

The ride home is full of laughter and shrieks of joy as the sound of Lil Waynes Got Money bumps out of the speakers. It was a good night and you are feeling on top of the world. There is nothing that could deflate your balloon, and for that moment, you feel as if everyone wants you and loves you.

Those daddy issues are just lying below the surface though, waiting until the next slow night to rear their ugly head.

Shit on my Stomach

The club was empty and I was on the stage. Times like this I could either practice some moved or twirl around. Nobody was at the stage. There were a few other girls working, although at this point all they were working was the bar. The bartender was the only one busy making drinks for the girls.

I looked at myself in the mirror that lined the wall, adjusting my top and pulling my fishnets up to the top of my thighs. I was bent over and heard the DJ whistle over the chorus of the song. I popped my head up and smiled into the mirror back at Al. He grinned back at me in the mirror.

As I sauntered across the stage towards the pole I watched my body move in the mirror. I lifted my hand up to touch the pole, grabbing on as I walked around it. There was something childish about twirling around the pole, swinging around like a little kid. I just happened to be clad in black fishnets, stripper heels, and something akin to a bikini as I did so.

Even after the months spent in the club I didn't know more than a basic climb up the pole. I would use it as a prop against my back to slide down while facing a customer, or twirl around it, but climbing up the pole scared me. Or was it falling down it that was the scary part.

Nobody was here, and I didn't mind. I didn't have to take my clothes off on the stage and as long as I kept moving the house mom didn't get upset. I slid down the pole and turned towards the DJ so my booty was facing the mirror while I was on my hands and knees. I tipped my head down to the floor and arched my hips back and forth, clapping my ass to the beat.

I put my head on the stage, looking back towards the mirror watching the way my ass shook. I played around on the floor for a little bit, sliding around the stage. It gets boring up there alone. The light peeped out when the door to the bathroom opened, and I saw my friend walk out. She came over to the stage and sat where I was dancing.

"Is there any money here yet?' She asked

"I havent made a dollar on this set yet. If it stays this way I'm gonna owe out of my own pocket tonight" I said between ass claps.

"If it doesn't pick up lets just leave early. We can sneak out."

"He's gonna be pissed if we do that again" I laughed. "You better ask first. Or at least get Al to say ok."

"Al is gonna want his money. I'd rather just owe him the next time we come in"

"Last time they said they would charge double if we skated out early. You may make that, but if I get hit with another night like tonight then I'm screwed."

"Ugh, okkkk. I'll go talk to Al after I take a walk."

"I have to finish this set, then I'll come with you." I rolled away over towards the pole, using the fishnets to help my slither across the stage.

I watched her get up and head over towards the bar. Someone must have had a customer in the back because there was a guy sitting at the bar now, and it was like watching piranhas realize there is blood in the water. Poor guy didn't stand a chance unless he left soon. He must have realized what was about to descend upon him as he grabbed his coat and headed for the door before my friend even made it half way to him.

As soon as the door closed Al came over the loud speaker "Now you all scared him away. Poor guy thought he was about to get eaten by all of you" He laughed into the mic as it shut off and the song played alone once again.

"Hey Al, can you play anything else besides this heavy metal for my sets, pleeease" I shouted over to him.

Al looked at me and laughed. I had one more song left to go and now he was going to play another heavy metal song. "Great" I muttered to myself. At least there wasn't anyone in here tonight. It was worse when I couldn't find the rhythm of the song and had to awkwardly move to a beat I didn't like.

Instead he one upped me and across the loud speaker I heard what every girl wants to hear while on stage.

"It's fun to stay at the Y.M.C.A" belted out across the club.

I stopped dead in my tracks as my jaw dropped. He was not really playing this. But he was.

Embracing the hilarity of the night, I started moving my arms above me in tune with the song.

"Y M C A" and my arms mimed along with the song.

The night must have gotten to everyone, because the rest of the girls and the bartender all started singing along performing the iconic dance.

Both Al and I started laughing. Wasn't this exactly what someone would expect to walk into at a strip club. The whole place erupting to YMCA with all of their clothes on, laughing hysterically.

The song came to an end and that meant I could hop down. We all had to do twenty minute stage sets tonight because it was so slow and so little girls. I gathered my things and jumped down. I saw that my friend had already made her way to Al and I was hoping it would go in our favor. The night was horrible. So much for working a Tuesday.

Al was smiling though, so that was a good thing. I started laughing as I got to him.

"That was amazing Al. So much better than the song you played before that."

"I usually save that for when the crowd gets a little unruly, but I haven't had to play it in awhile and figured we could all use the laugh." He said.

"Nicely done." I replied.

"So Al, think we can head out soon. The night is dead and you know we have a shitty drive." She batted her eyelashes up at him. Al wasn't a first timer though, and he was all but immune to most feminine charms. Thats what happens when you watch them dance naked all the time.

"Tell you what" Al started "I'll let you go home after your next set. You just have to make sure that you remember me when its a good night."

"HEY AL"

We all turned to look back at the private dance area, which had two girls coming over from it.

"If you had to share your biggest fantasy what would it be?"

My friend and I looked at each other, wondering if he would answer it and where this conversation had started. The two girls were clearly continuing a conversation, although I wasn't sure where it was headed.

"Natalies man told her that he wanted to try out a golden shower today before she came in" The blonde said, jerking her thumb towards the girl next to her. "We're talking about kinks. What's yours?"

We stood there, not a part of the conversation but a part of it.

"I want a girl to take a shit on my chest. I just haven't found one to do it yet."

The blonde looked at him then at Natalie, "there ya go. He one upped you."

"He wants me to piss on him and I don't know if I can do it."

I knew my eyebrows had to be raised at this point. I couldn't leave the booth yet, but I was hoping we faded into the background. I didn't have anything to add to this conversation.

"Put down some towels, or grab one of those waterproof blankets made for squirters. There's something about the warmth that is just nice." Al advised them.

My friend and I looked at each other, again, and then back. "We're gonna go pack up now Al. Thank you!" We both extricated ourselves from the continuing conversation.

It only took a minute before we found ourselves back in the dressing room. "What the fuck was that"

I said, to fits of laughter. "I just can't believe he admits to that. I didn't think I would admit that but ok."

"Did we really just here that conversation?" My friend said.

"Yes, and I can never unhear it either. Let's pack up and get the fuck out of here." I said.

It never took as long to pack up as it did to get ready. By this point it was just taking off all the slutty clothes, the foot molding heels, and putting on comfortable sweat pants and a baggy top. We wouldn't wash our faces until we got home.

Here we both were, faces made up as if we were going on a photo shoot dressed in sweat pants and sweat shirts with sneakers on. Nothing to see here.

I threw my clothes in my bag, and hit the ladies room one more time before we left. It would be another long ride home, made even longer with no money in my pocket.

I'll Bet You $20.00

I was walking around the club for a little while. It was a busy night and the place was packed with not only customers but also girls. This club was made for money and people. I walked around the main stage, and ventured into the front of the building. The lower floor had two main rooms, with a staircase and a stage in the front room and the main stage in the second room. There was a smaller room off to the side of the main stage for private dances.

I was in the front room near the door walking back towards the stairs. My feet hurt and I didn't like the girls working. I wanted to get upstairs and take a break for a little while. The girls tonight were the mean girls; I couldn't tell if they were the popular girls, or the ugly ducklings that found themselves. Either way it was like I was cheerleading back in high school; we didn't like each other but we were all there for the same reason.

I hated these damn stairs. The last thing I want to do in eight inch platform shoes is traverse a set of stairs. It reminded me of a grand entrance that a debutante would make heading to the ball. Here I was trying to stay elegant in stilettos, fishnets and dental floss artfully arranged to appear alluring. Upstairs there were chairs I could sit in and take just a moment to not have to be "on".

Not many people came upstairs, and if they did they were going to the VIP section or the dressing room. I walked up the last of the stairs and when I looked up, of course there would be a couple of guys sitting in the chairs. I sighed to myself, as this was literally the last thing that I wanted right now.

I walked into the dressing room off to the left instead of heading towards the comfy chairs. I would go pee and then come back out, hopefully they would be gone by the time that I got back out. The bathrooms were at the end of the vanity tables, and now that I was out of view I hobbled over towards them.

Part of the house fee went towards the stocking of supplies in the bathroom. Here was a cache of supplies that might be needed during the night: razors, pads, tampons. Q-tips, baby wipes, mouth wash and tooth brushes. We could buy other items, like outfits and stockings.

I slid my panties and bikini bottoms down over my fishnets and plopped down on the toilet to pee. By this time in the night my feet were throbbing to the beat of the music. The heels were actually pretty comfortable, but it was simply being on them for hours whilst dancing and cavorting around the bar.

I wiped front to back, carefully checking to make sure I didn't decide to keep a memento of toilet paper for when I went back downstairs. I grabbed a wipe and went over the vagina one more time. There was nothing more embarrassing than a little white ball of toilet paper reflecting back under the black light as you were trying to be sultry and seductive for money.

Satisfied with the results, I threw the wipe away and just sat for a moment while I air dried. That was the thing about wipes, it didn't feel good walking away sliding in your panties. Had it been enough time where they may have left or should I just sit here a bit longer.

The eight inch heels made for an awkward standup as my knees were at an unfamiliar angle. I got up, flushing the toilet and pulling everything back up, situating the layers of lingerie. I checked everything in the mirror, making sure my outfit was ok. The lighting in here wasn't made to look at makeup, so I would stop by my bag and freshen up before heading back out.

Once that was all set I made my way back out to the public area. The guys were gone, I sighed in relief as it gave me a place to sit. The chairs in the dressing room weren't meant for lounging, whereas these were made to be sat in.

Sitting down, I breathed out, thinking about how little money I had made. It was busy sure, there were lots of people, but there were also lots of girls and that meant competition. Friday nights were always a different clientele for me also. The guys that were out were not looking to spend money, they were here to celebrate or pre-game, but rarely was it to come and drop bills.

The laughter came first, followed by the heads coming up the stairs. "Damnit." I muttered to myself. They were coming back. I straightened a little but didn't bother to get up. They had drinks in their hand, fresh drinks. They had went to the bar. They got to the chairs before they noticed me.

'Hi" one of them said

"Hi, how are you" I smiled and said to them.

"You don't mind if we join you, do you?" the other asked.

"I think you guys were here first, so do you mind if I join you guys?"

"A beautiful girl, why would that be a bother to us?" the same guy said.

"Good, because my feet hurt and I really didn't want to get up." I laughed.

"how is your night going so far?" Guy number one piped up.

"its ok, I'm just taking a break from the crowd downstairs. I can't believe how many people there are and it gets to be so hot."

"We come here a lot on Friday's and this is pretty normal" said guy number two. "We haven't seen you here before though?"

"No, this is my first Friday working. My friend and I usually work at another club on Friday's."

"What's your name?"

"Mallory" I replied.

"Well that's not a stripper name. Is that your real name?"

"its not, but I liked the name. Ironically my friends real name is a stripper name but she won't use it."

"No way, what is her name" guy number one asked.

"Her name is Diamond"

"Her REAL name" emphasizing real, "her real name is Diamond? There is no way her mother did that to her."

"No, it really is."

"What is wrong with her mother? Thats not possible.'

"I'll bet you twenty dollars that her name is Diamond. Legal name".

"I'll give you twenty dollars if you can prove that."

I laughed. Slapping my hands down on the arms of the chair, I heaved myself as gracefully as I could muster onto my heel clad feet.

"I'll be right back" I told them.

I knew she kept her ID tucked away in her things at that nights makeup station. I went to retrieve it, the dressing room being on the same floor and a quick walk away.

I returned within four minutes, and sat down in a huff. I covered her address and showed them her name. And there it was in government form.

"Pay up" I laughed, holding out my hand.

They sat there in shock, not that I was right but more of who would do that to their kid. I laughed, good old Italian boys; they might be a little shocked at name choices but they honored their bets. They paid me twenty. We kept talking for awhile and then they got up to leave.

"Thanks for a decent conversation tonight. That's why we came up here, we couldn't take the vapid air headed conversations trying to get money. Here's a little sack of some bud, for your ride home tonight".

I happily accepted the gift. "You know you came to a strip club where everyone here is trying to make money?"

"Ya, but its the rudeness when you don't want to spend it on that girl that kills the vibe."

"I suppose" I said.

I stood up as well, and headed to the dressing room to put away the ID and the now illegal contraband I had on me.

"You guys have a good night" I smiled at them as they headed down the staircase. Sleep was starting to creep at the back of my head, and I decided I didn't want to go back downstairs. The night was almost over and I didn't have any stage sets left that I had to be on.

The Girls

They were a snotty, I'm better than you, type. I always liked to people watch, which is a proper way of say stare at everyone else. Tonight there was a redhead who had bright red lipstick and walked around with a smile plastered to her face. Her bouncy curls and cheery face made her seem like the girl next door ; in the fifties she would have been working as a grocery store cashier you wouldn't mind getting directions from. Upstairs she scowled like a prima Donna bitch that just smelled something she didn't like. If she were the only person around and you were lost you may opt to stay that way rather than ask for directions. I always liked watching the different personalities come out when they got near customers.

There was also a blonde who was older. She was very tan and beautiful, but was closer to forty-five or fifty. She was wearing black leather high heeled boots, that went up over her knees to about mid thigh. She had big perky boobs, the kind that came from an early boob job where the implant was there to just be large but not necessarily look real. Her skin was pulled taut over them, and she was getting the wrinkles on her chest in between her machine guns. The first time I had seen her she was pulling on knee pads that couldn't even be seen once she had those boots on.

"My knees can't take the stage anymore" she had said to me. "I slide these on under the boots and now I can move all around the stage and nobody knows anything." I had to marvel at her ingenuity to keep going.

One night this older girl, meaning at least in her thirties came and sat next to me. She was running late rushing to get dressed. Her hair was already done; she donned a long blonde ponytail that sat high atop her head. She was talking to the house mom about what she had to make that night.

"I need 1600 tonight. I have Joshies birthday party this week and I said yes to this gift."

"You'll make that no problem." The house mom said. "Go sit in the VIP lounge and you'll make that in no time.

The VIP lounge I thought to myself. I didn't know we could sit up there. I had done a few champagne rooms upstairs but I didn't know the bar was open for us to sit around and wait. Maybe it wasn't open to everyone. She clearly had worked there for some time. I hadn't seen her before, but the house mom was talking to her like they were friends, assuring her that she could make that much tonight.

I wondered how she was gonna make it, because I didn't see the clientele needed for that kind of money.

Amanda looked about twelve. She was tiny and petite, little perky boobs and slim hips. She was short even with heels on, and always wore the same type of outfit. Leg warmers over her black heels, an open sweater around her to keep her warm that was always over a bikini style outfit.

What threw me was that she was always eating dinner at the bar, typically with some old customer. Always, as in every time I saw her. In the dressing room she would talk about her little sister being under her care now that their parents were gone. She didn't talk much beyond that.

I didn't see her on the stage very often, and if I did her customer would monopolize her time up there so she didn't have to parade around the stage much. She had one or two customers who would come in for her for most of the night. Never on the same night, but rather like a rotation. Both of them were in their sixties, if not older. Treated her to dinner each night they came in and then brought her back to the private room after time spent at the bar.

I have to admit, it was envious. Dealing with one or two old men who fed you and bought you things. Not a bad gig. She knew she had it good too. She guarded her men like she was a hawk and they were two little mice she was going to pluck out of a field. One night she had gotten up and went to the rest room (which was also the dressing room), and while away my friend walked by her customer at the bar, stopping to chat with him.

When Amanda came walking back up, she sat down in her seat, which was on the opposite side of where my friend now stood. Her customer abruptly turned his attention back to Amanda, signaling the end of any conversation they may have been engaged in.

I watched this from my stage set, wondering what may happen later. The look on Amandas face was one that said she wouldn't forget what just occurred.

And she didn't. Later that night we were all in the dressing room getting ready to go home when Amanda stormed in, throwing the door against the wall with how hard she pushed it. She went over to her locker, which none of us new girls had, and started getting undressed. "Don't try to poach my fucking customer again." She said. It wasn't loud, but it was definitely clear and menacing. I didn't bother to engage as my friend retorted back to her. I kept packing my stuff up, I was tired and just wanted to go home.

Mental Intoxication

I don't think many people set out on their career path aiming to be a dancer. At least I didn't. What I will say is that there is something about the power that is held when you are on the stage with your body writhing and men and women staring at you with pure carnal lust in their eyes. It is a boost to the serotonin levels when someone will throw endless amounts of money on you. Or selects you out of a room full of women to spend their hard earned money on you. When someone walks up to the stage with no other intent than to spend money. It is intoxicating to move and flow, to feel the power of money raining over your body.

I slide my naked flesh over the floor and I can feel the string on my underwear lift up as a bill slides under and the underwear snap back. I look back over my shoulder at the person who placed it there and I grin. I fold myself over, my knees are spread apart and they are behind me asI fold my shoulder down to the ground and look back at them upside down. I run my hands over my robust butt. I see the bills fly down over my ass. I shake my ass more, picking my head up and arching my back, The money still flows and now there is a collection on the stage. I bring my knees together, and I slide forward so I am flat on my stomach. I lift one leg up in the air as I turn onto my hip, caressing my skin once more.

My customer looks at me with hunger in his eyes, and it feeds the greedy exhibitionist inside of me. I slide around on money and I can't help but want more.

Moving back towards the edge of the stage, I pick my underwear up just a little. I hold my breath as I look into the eyes of this person, the corners of my mouth twitch up because we both know I have him, and we both like the roles we are each playing. Cat and mouse, vampire and victim, exhibitionist and voyeur.

My song came to and end and I snapped out of the hold the music held on me. Looking around I had to grab all the money that had been thrown at me. I had more than just ones, with a twenty tucked into my underwear. I smiled, thanked the face and kept it moving.

I gathered the money, picked up my discarded clothing and clutched it all to my naked chest as I walked off the stage and into the dressing room. Here I organized my money and sat in my thongs for a minute. I grabbed a baby wipe off the pack that lived on the counter and wiped down my arms and legs. I sat for a minute and rolled my shoulders back. That set was a good haul, but most of mine were.

The stage and I were friends. As much of an introvert that I was, for some reason once the initial fright of a brand new stage went away, I owned the time I was up there. I wasn't the top money maker in the club, but few rivaled the amount of money I made on the stage. When I would walk on that stage it was like a whole different person emerged, and any fear of being naked in front of people disappeared. It was very rare that I was not sober, apart from smoking weed on the way in to the club. I didn't need to drink, in fact it made me sloppy.

I wanted a clear head to focus on my money and what was going on around me. The mental intoxication that I gained from simply rolling around in money was enough to bolster my confidence better than any shot of tequila could. It hadn't always been that way though. In the beginning I would drink along with the customers.

Its not always the girls that you have to worry about robbing you, but the guys will try to get away with so much more if they think that you are drunk.

It may be a wayward hand, a lewd offer, or trying to mess with your money. I hated the moment that I had to question if I had really just witnessed a guy try to take money from me on the stage. It was easier to just be sober.

You're Different

It was a slow night, and there were a lot of girls. I should say, it was a slow night for me. I was at a new club with my friend and I was not doing as good as I hoped I would. I had only been on the stage once in a few hours, which was rare, but there were that many girls where I didnt have to.

I was doing The Circuit around the club and stopped at the bar to grab a soda. I liked to get a Shirley temple, and if anyone said anything I could say it was a dirty Shirley. It wasn't likely to happen, but I had a plan. I was sitting there sipping my soda, perched on the stool looking over the club. I sat upright with my back straight so the stomach rolls didn't rear their ugly head. Everyone has the rolls, no matter their size, I just didn't want mine on display in the little outfit I had on. I tried to smile outward, seem approachable to the guys that were there.

I scanned the room and was taking note of how people acted, who talked to who, the girls that were making money and with whom.

I had turned down a lot of offers for more than just dancing at this club, more so than usual. When a customer asks you for something sexual, and you refuse, usually he doesn't leave. He just looks for another girl who will say yes. I paid attention to who went with them, it made it easier to know when it would be a slow night for money.

Whenever there were girls working who sold more than dancing, who were fucking and sucking in the back, it would be a shitty night. I sighed and sipped my soda. One of the bouncers from the door came over, which was a usual occurrence. A dancer always wants to be friends with the door staff, as they will either help in a problem or keep the problems away from you.

"Hey Phil, hows it going tonight?" I asked him.

"Hiya Mallory, whaddaya drinking"

"Ehh, just a Shirley temple. I'm not much of a drinker."

He looked at me a little funny when I said that, and I laughed.

"what is that look for?" I said, chuckling.

He didn't answer me and I let it go. Phil wasn't that much of a talker, at least not to me. I still tried though.

Sighing, I said "its slow for me tonight. I feel like it shouldn't be with as many people as there are. but there's a lot of girls too."

Silence. I sipped my soda again.

"I like to people watch. You see some interesting things when you just sit quietly and observe." I tried again with the conversation. This time I must have caught his attention.

"In all the time I have worked here I mostly just sit and watch. All social norms go out the window in a place like this. I have seen so many things, things you wouldn't even think of." Then he turned pointedly towards me and said "but you're different. Sure I hear the stories, the claims of going to school and needing tuition money, but you. You're not telling a lie when you tell your "real" story."

I looked at Phil with interest. Sure I wanted conversation, but only to help pass the time. Not for a character assessment, but I pushed. "Oh, and what makes you say that?"

"The way you carry yourself. The money you don't make. The customers you turn down but others don't. The genuine way that you interact with people. You're not drinking and you're not heading for the bathroom. You're not built for this industry."

Now I was the one who didn't have much to say. I ignored the silence by taking another sip of my soda.

"I think I'm up on stage next" I said, more out of courtesy to extricate myself from the conversation.

"I'll see you later, Phil. Have a good night"

"You too, Mallory. Hope you make good money but it looks like a tough crowd tonight."

I laughed.

"That it is, that it is. Let's see how the stage goes."

And with that, I was off.

Center Stage

We were working at one of the sister clubs tonight. The owners of the main club we worked at had maybe four other clubs spread out around the city. In order to work at the main club, you had to work two days at the other clubs. They didn't say it, but they were assigned based on how you looked. The clubs had different clientele, different vibes and experiences. The music would be different, as well as the level of scuzziness that you would feel walking in.

This night was a "volunteer" night; the club was short girls and although we had already put in two nights at one of the clubs we offered to work at this one tonight when the house mom had called earlier. She had given us directions, told us where to park, and then who we should ask for when we got there.

"Where the fuck is this place, in the ghetto?" my friend said as we parked the car. The lot had an attendant for the girls coming in to work, and made sure they had both parking and a safe walk inside.

"I haven't ever been to this side of the city. Hopefully its a good night." I said. We had just finished smoking the routine two blunts before work, and stepped out of the car. Luckily we had rolled the windows down ahead of time, otherwise we would have had a cloud of smoke to greet the man in the parking lot. The clubs could be funny about the smell of weed for some reason. They looked the other way for girls that were blowing coke up their nose in the bathrooms or falling down drunk; but show up smelling like weed and it was a huge problem. I just didn't get it.

We grabbed our bags and headed inside, walking over the gravel parking lot. I hated this part the most, walking into a new club. So many questions raced through my mind; what is the stage like? How many songs on a set? How are the other girls? Are they fucking and sucking in the back? Is the DJ nice? What kind of music do they play? What kind of music won't they play? My nerves and anxiety were kicking into full gear, but there wasn't time for that. I needed to make some money, which was the whole point for working the extra night. Rent was due.

The door swung open and into the dark we went. It was always an adjustment to the eye going inside the clubs. It could be the day shift, bright as can be outside, and when you walk behind that door it turns into midnight at the disco real quick. The music hit first, it was some rap song.

Oh boy I thought to myself, this should be interesting. Most of the clubs wont play rap because they don't want to have fights and its not really fitting the vibe of sexiness and fantasies. The doorman was the first to greet us, to check IDs for normal customers.

"We're here to work tonight" my friend said.

"Marissa sent us over. Said you were short on the schedule" I said.

He looked us over, noted the bags, and pointed behind him to another door. "Head inside ladies. There is a stairwell on the left. Head upstairs to the dressing room. The DJ will be up to get your names, and give you stage information."

We headed in and went up the stairs. At the top landing we walked back a little, and into a wide open room. In here there was a round kitchen table with a few chairs, a microwave, fridge, and a ton of lockers with makeup tables. We found two empty spots and set our things down. I looked around and spotted a bathroom, where I went to go pee before getting dressed.

When I came out, I started setting my stuff up. Straightener, check. I plugged it in to start heating up while I began on my makeup. I hated doing my makeup. I was never any good at it, and never was able to look as flawless as the other girls. I got by with some eye makeup but never went in for the full face effect. Nevertheless, putting on my work face never took me as long as the other girls.

My go-to hair style was to just straighten it. If I tried curls they never lasted, so I straightened my hair and then let the night do with it as it pleased. I made sure to keep anything that smelled strongly, or had glitter, off of me. Most guys didnt want to get a dance from someone that would leave tell tale signs of it when they went home.

While we were getting dressed the DJ came up, and gave us the same spiel that we got from the other club. "We rode together, so can you put us on the same stage set so we can leave together?" My friend asked.

"Single stage sets tonight, but I'll let you guys be on the hour and the first quarter as a thank you for coming in but I need you down there for the next set starting at 7. Last set starts at 1. House fee is also waived but its normally twenty plus tip to the DJ. Payable before you leave. What's your genre? I play a little rap early at night but wont play it once people start to come in. And I need your names."

Once he had left I started picking through my clothes. I would start with black to be discreet. If I needed to I would throw on something with color once I felt a bit more comfortable with the layout. We didn't look around much when we first walked in, so I wasn't sure what we were dealing with. New stage, new layout, hopefully new money tonight.

I picked out my black thongs, fishnet thigh-highs, black bathing suit- like booty shorts, and a black triangle top. My shoes were black, and they completed the look. I rolled the fishnets up my thighs first, these would stay on all night even when everything else came off. Thongs then shorts, followed by the top, and I was done.

I sat down and strapped my shoes on. We always walked down together, so I waited for her to finish. I picked up the straightener and took care of a couple wispy hairs I noticed while staring in the mirror. I was nervous, but there was no time for anxiety or nerves. She finished getting ready and it was show time.

We headed for the stairwell, which was dingy and tight. It was clearly not for customers to come up, as it wasn't inviting to anyone. It was narrow, forcing us to go down single file. There was one light that was at the top of the stairs where the landing was. The vibe in here was abandoned old mill building. When we got to the bottom, we opened the door into the vibe of night club.

The lights were dim, the music was bumping, and the strobe was going. The black lights near the door let the entering party know they were headed in for some fun. The floor was carpeted once we got past the entrance, and thats when we realized where the clubs name came from. In the center of the club was the largest stage we had seen yet. You could walk completely around it, with chairs set up around the perimeter. The bar was off to the left, and the partition for the private dances was in the back right of the club. This place was literally a stage, with a little bit of gathering room. The DJ had a home along the back wall, there was a spot for private dances and that was it.

We made our way over to the bar. It was always the first place to go when you wanted to look like you had intent but really just wanted to look around. Wait for the bartender, order a drink, wait for the drink, pay, wait for the change. This whole transaction could take up to twenty minutes depending on how busy the place was.

Not only did we get a chance to stand there, avoiding the awkward feeling of being the new kid at lunch time with nowhere to sit, the customers got a chance to see you. The regulars would always notice if you were new, and inevitably someone would come and make conversation while waiting.

Tonight that would not be the case however. While initiating step one of the procedure, waiting for the bartender, we turned and purview the clientele for the moment. Like two lionesses scoping out the Serengeti for what might possible be on the dinner menu that evening, we scanned the club. It was nearly empty.

We looked at each other.

"Its still early, we don't usually get out this early."

"Let's hope. I'll be fucking pissed if I drove here tonight and its for no fucking money" my friend said.

We looked at the bartender, who was sitting at the other end of the stage talking to a regular. She wasn't in any rush. Great, I thought to myself. Another one of those bartenders. These women were such bitches and for no reason. They were friendly to the customers but then treated the dancers like they were vying for the same paycheck.

With what some of these bartenders wore I sometimes questioned if they were making their own money on the side. This one had on her own fishnet stockings, short black shorts, a black corset that held her voluptuous boobs perked up. She had her bottle blonde hair in an updo, with thick makeup on. Pretty, and likely making a good amount of money in tips.

I looked up to the stage and tried to not let my mouth hang open. Climbing the pole was the first dancer I had ever seen that was plus size. She was perfectly evenly proportioned, and while she wasn't fat in the traditional sense she was far from skinny. Her body was tight and toned, and although large one could say that she was just big boned. She turned and I noticed that she was gorgeous, with smooth alabaster skin.

She had beautiful dark curly hair that cascaded over her shoulders and down her back as she lifted her right hand over her head gaining a higher grasp on the pole as she slid her knees up the pole. I watched as she clasped the pole between her thick knees, and raised herself up to a standing position.

She repeated the process, this time with her left arm lifting her up as she inched up the pole. Her routine began once she got to a height that worked for the tricks she was about to perform. I sat in amazement as I watched her move her body round and round, up and down, upside down and right side up.

All of the thoughts I had on who could pole dance went out the window in that one, three minute song. Her body moved so gracefully and fluidly and seemingly without effort. Climbing the pole and dancing on it required so much physical strength that it seemed out of reach for anyone who didn't strength train. At the very least one has to be able to life their own body.

I could barely lift my own frame, and yet there was this other dancer with thighs as thick as my head who made this look effortless.

Frankly it was also a shock to see her working. I could tell this was not the diamond in the clubs portfolio based on that alone. They would have never let her work at the main club, with the stereotypical stripper look that they were trying to attain there.

It becomes quite apparent after working in the sex industry for a little while that there is a different body type for every customer. While her body type may not be for the majority of the customers, she was and did, make money in the place she was in.

She was good at pole dancing and had a stack of money on the stage, so it was clear this wasn't her first night working. While surprising to see her working, it made me feel better about where we were for the night.

Working in a club that always has the same body type could make it either a really bad night or a really good night. The main club usually had women that had big boobs and little much else. Which did not fit my body type, which is the exact opposite. I have no boobs and a big butt. Depending on the customers for the night I could make a good amount of money or be the oddity that just wasn't a hit on the menu that night.

If she was working in this club, that would mean that the customer base would have a palette that wasn't so bland and without seasoning. If we kept coming to this club, the money may prove to be worth it.

Who Wears Short Shorts

I sauntered back to the private dance area, which was really just a bunch of chairs behind a partition of lattice fencing. My customer for this dance as a younger guy, very average in appearance. He was pretty handsome, so I was surprised by his cool, quiet demeanor. And his outfit of choice.

From the waist up he was normal, in a t-shirt. From the waist down he was in short, thin athletic shorts. From initial appearances one would think he was out for a healthy jog with the running shoes and shorts on. The fact that he took a left into the strip club and it was dusk told me he was here to try to get off.

He didn't waste time agreeing to a dance with me; he had sat at the stage during my set and when I got off I walked around to see if he wanted a dance. We were headed back there now. I let him pick the chair once we got past the white lattice. He headed for the chair that would get the least amount of people walking by. He wanted a bit of privacy.

I let him sit down and then I waited for the current song to end. This way I was starting right at the beginning and he didn't feel cheated. I always started my private dances standing up, and then as the song wore on I moved closer to them. There was also a matter of pride, I didn't want someone to think in their head that I was a bad dancer.

There were times that didn't matter, like if they were obnoxious, belligerent, to hands on, or asking for what I wasn't offering. Other times I had to just deal with whatever they were pitching to me because I needed the money.

This guy wanted me to sit down on his lap, with my back to him, and rub my ass over his crotch. I tried to lift myself up as much as I could so that I didn't feel anything that was poking through the thin layer of his shorts. Ironically, trying to stay away from him only made me feel more gross as now it was clear as to what I was touching.

I stood up, dancing as I did so, my hips moving to the music. I smiled down at him, and moved in a little closer. I stood away as long as I could manage, before he reached up for my wrist to bring me in closer.

"Eh eh" I scolded him, wagging my finger and backing away as I smirked at him with a devilish look on my face. I pushed him back in his seat and turned around so my ass was facing him. I sighed to myself, hoping this delay would bring me another dance and another twenty dollars.

I bent over, my ass high up in the air because of the heels. I rubbed my hands over the backs of my legs, up my ass cheeks, and then grabbed them and pulled them apart. I had my thongs on still so he wasn't seeing what he wanted, but he could imagine. I heard him groan just as the song ended. I smiled back coyly,

"Do you want another dance?" I asked him.

He pulled one hundred dollars from his sock and put that on the small table where my drink was resting.

"Keep going" he said quietly.

As the next song was already underway, I just kept moving my ass cheeks around bent over in front of him. He kept staring.

I stood up, turned around, and moved in closer to him. I put my right leg on the outside of his on the seat cushion, and let my left leg slide down in between his. I was sitting on him, but my thigh was in between his legs and I could control where my hips went better. I started pushing myself up and down using the foot that was still on the floor. I let his face settle in between my chest.

His hands were politely resting on my lower back, I knew he felt the sweatiness of working. My feet were starting to hurt and I wanted this to be over. It was easy to just keep moving and keep his head below my face. I peek through the lattice work looking at what else was happing in the club, still dancing.

I had realized that he didn't want to look at me, this was solely for him to feel the touch of a woman.

When the song ended I could feel his demeanor change. I looked down and he quietly told me that he was all set for the next song. "Thank you." he said to me.

"Oh, you're welcome." I smiled at him. He was young, and even if he was a little weird at least he was closer to my age than the other creeps who came in with the running shorts.

I stood up, and he said "you can keep the whole hundred even though we only did two songs."

"Oh, thank you!" I exclaimed in surprise. That usually never happens, especially not with the younger guys.

He adjusted his shorts as he stood up. He didn't wait for me, but instead made right towards the exit of the private dance area. I wasn't sure if I had upset him, or he wasn't happy. I didn't think it was either, given the tip he just left me, but they at least usually wait to walk out together.

I peeked though the lattice and watched him walk right towards the exit of the club. The door swung open, with the ray of daylight piercing the illusion of it being nighttime inside. I guess that was that for the mystery running man in short shorts.

$300.00

I leaned my weight on my shoulder and palms as I shook my hips front and back, jiggling my ass to the music. I was on stage with a couple other girls, and luckily the chairs around it were relatively packed.

My black thigh-high fishnet stockings were a staple at this point, staying on even if everything else came off. I was down to my black thongs; also another must have item in my wardrobe. My top was off to the side with the bottoms that I would wear walking around, and the stack of money I had made on the current set so far.

The other two girls on stage were engrossed with their customers of the moment, but the old guy I was dancing for just wasn't paying out as much anymore. If the club was busy I danced until they either stopped putting money out, or if I saw that someone else was offering me more than a few ones. When I popped my head up, now I was sitting on the stage with my legs forming the shape of an 'M', I use the opportunity to shake my hair down my back and scan the stage for money placed on the rail.

Directly across from me I noticed a man and woman, each with a five dollar bill out. They were looking right at me, and when they saw that I noticed them they smiled and moved the money closer. I had to wrap things up from the spot I was in; I turned and smiled to the customer

"Thanks sweetie, I'll see you around tonight I hope" winking on the word hope. I grabbed the dollar bill he had out, tucked it in my thong and then picked up the clothes and money I already had. I stood up, and sauntered over to the couple.

Smiling as I got closer, I didn't waste time with the sultry seduction that I normally would have started with. I was already virtually naked, dropping the clothes back behind me. You never wanted your money close to the edge of the stage while you were dancing. I had seen customers actually take from a girls stash and give it back to her while she was dancing, as if it were his own.

I kneeled along the edge of the stage, in a table top position along the drink rail. I was mindful of where my foot went, careful to not kick someone or a drink. That would ruin any money to be made real quick. I arched my back, and crawled up a little bit; it was nice when there were a group of paying customers, because it gave me more space to work with. I could crawl, or lay down along the edge rather than being confined to the width of one person. People don't want to share what their paying for unless its with a friend or a spouse.

I grabbed the five from both of them as I inched my way up the bar, tucking it into my thong alongside the one from the last customer. I hit the girl in the face with the bounce back of shaking my hips again, her chin along the small of my back. I smiled at her as I stretched along the bar, my back coming down onto the table top this time, my hands caressing my ribs as I looked up at her partner.

"Hi guys, hows the night so far" I asked them.

"We're having a great time" She said to me.

I sat up just as she put another five down in front of her, so I moved closer to her as I sat up. This time I mimicked a crab, where I put my feet down closer to her but rested my weight on my hands behind me. My knees were close to her head as I gyrated my hips around for her. He put a bunch of ones down in front of her while I danced.

It was clear that while they were both there, the point was for her to get the show while he watched. At least for the time being. I used one of the ones he set down and put it inside her shirt; she was pretty busty so the dollar bill sat nicely and didn't move much. I used my teeth to grab the bill from in between her boobs. Her man put more money down, clearly enjoying the small show.

It was always fun when the women came in, because they usually were not lesbians or even bisexual. They were there to do something crazy with their spouses, or liven up their bedroom routine, and sometimes, they were there to play out a scene.

I found out shortly after that sometimes women come to make it easier for the couple to find a playmate. As I was dancing for her, she leaned in and asked me

"Will you come home with us. We will pay you three hundred dollars to have sex with us tonight"

I was happy that my face was not looking at her, because I was speechless at the offer. I had never had a couple ask me to go home with them.

"Oh, I don't do that kind of thing" I replied. "I come here to dance and go home, but I'm sure you can find one of the other girls to take you up on that offer".

I knew at that point they would not be spending anymore money on me, and I moved to collect the bills that were still on the stage. I tucked it all away, and they sat back. I gathered my clothes just as I realized that the song was coming to an end and my stage set was over. I smiled at them, "Thanks, have a good night", I said as I stood up in my heels.

I traipsed off the stage, hands full of money and clothes. I had bills tucked in my thong so I stopped at the stairs leading off the stage. I pulled the bills out of my thongs, and continued walking to the dressing room. This was the only time I walked almost bare-assed around the club, heading off the stage and back to the dressing room.

Once I got back there I found my friend. She was sitting near our stuff on her phone.

"You're never going to believe what this couple just did?!" I burst out.

She looked up at me, "what?"

"They offered me three hundred dollars to go home with them for the night and have sex with them!"

"Was it that Brazilian couple that you were just dancing with for on stage?" She countered.

"Ya! I didn't know they were Brazilian though."

"I heard them talking with the bartender when they came in, and she is from Brazil. And all they offered was three hundred? Lame."

"I was a little shocked that was all they offered, not that I would have taken it anyways." I paused. " I've never really thought about what price I would need to go home with someone. Or if there even is a price."

"I just know it's definitely not three hundred." I said laughing. I was counting the money I had just made on stage. "They did give me like thirty dollars on stage, so there's that at least."

"Cheap mother fuckers. They probably spent that money on stage hoping you would go home with them. Then all they offered was three hundred." She said. She was in a grumpy ass mood, and based on her phone in her hand she wasn't making any money.

"I'm glad this night is almost over. I'm not doing my last stage set. There isn't even anyone here except for the fucking couple and old guys not spending money. Everyone cleared out while you were dancing for them, and now they wont spend unless its to leave with someone." She ranted, while digging through her bag.

"Did you pay out already? I have to go do that still. I'm gonna pay house and DJ and then I'll be back. That was my last set so if you want to leave after we can. I had sorted all the money that I had just made on stage and put it with the money made earlier in the night. I broke off the house fee and the tip for the DJ.

I left my thongs and thigh highs on as I slipped on the bottoms over my heels. I tied the top around in back, and set off to pay out. The music smacked me in the face as soon as I opened the door; funny how a door can be such a simple barrier.

I meandered over to the DJ, handing him his portion for the night.

"Thanks doll" he said to me "See you soon, Mallory"

"You're welcome love. Hey, have you seen Alicia?"

"She was just sitting at the other side of the bar."

"Thanks Mikey! Have a great night."

After stepping off the DJ platform I meandered to the other side of the bar and sure enough thats where she was. I handed her the money for working that night. I didn't linger long because I didn't want her to ask me where my friend was. She could get out of her last set if she was dancing for someone, hopefully she didn't go looking when only two girls were on stage.

I walked back into the dressing room to find her changed into street clothes and ready to go. Sweat pants and a t-shirt. The classic attire for someone who wears lingerie and heels all night long.

"I just paid out, let me change real quick before Alicia comes looking for you." I ripped my heels off, rolled my thigh-highs down, peeled my thongs off and pulled the strings on my top then threw them all in the bag. I dug out my sweats and t-shirt and threw those on. I rounded the transformation out by throwing my sneakers on. Apart from the hair and makeup, a stark contrast to the clothes I now wore, someone couldn't tell what I had been doing all night.

We heaved the bags over our shoulders and made a bee-line for the door. Luckily we could sneak out the back door here, which not many clubs offered. The trick was to not look back, even if you heard your name. It could be a customer, another dancer, or the house mom we were dodging. Either way, not turning around meant you could feign ignorance the next encounter and still get away in the moment.

The walk back to the car was brisk and short. She had her keys out and unlocked the door right as we got close so not to draw attention when the lights blinked for the alarm. I didn't even stop to throw my bag in the back seat, opting to keep it with me while I climbed in to make a quicker get away.

We were both buckling our seat belts as she dropped the shifter into reverse, and just like that the night was over. "I have to get gas and I'm hungry. Can you roll something up when we stop." She said.

"Sure can. I'll come in with you, i'm hungry too. I didn't eat anything tonight."

She parked and we walked in to the gas station. The clerk looked at us once, and then did a double take. We may have looked like we were ready for bed, but the makeup on our faces was a stark contrast to that. My hair was still straight, her hair was still bouncy curls, and the dramatic eye makeup we had both opted for screamed night club.

I ignored his looks as I walked back and grabbed a drink and a few snacks for the road. I got to the counter and asked for a pack of cigars also. He didn't card me, but I wasn't surprised at that, being so late and looking as we did. Salty and sweet with a bottle of soda and I headed back to the car with my pack of Mango Games.

I could at least empty the cigars while we were still near a garbage can. I set to work getting ready to roll up for the long ride we had ahead of us. Two blunts would be good enough I thought. Worst case I think there was a broken cigar in the door I could mend if needed, depending on how bad the night had been.

The Fight

We stopped at the usual pizza place that was on the way to the group of clubs we worked at. The pizza was delicious and so were the boys behind the counter, which made for great eye candy and a full belly. A small cheese pizza was the usual, every once in awhile we may spice it up and add some fries, but it was usually pizza. A blunt before and a blunt after and we were ready to get the night started.

We had opted to work at one of the downtown clubs tonight, as the money had been good the last time we were told to work there. Lately it seemed that way, at least for us. The main club just hadn't been bringing in the money like this one, so we seemed to be spending more and more time here.

We figured it may have been new girl luck, but that can only be used so long before you're not the new girl. Whenever we went into a new club we would make great money on the first few nights we worked. The line would be something like

"hi, I'm new here, wanna help me make some money on my first night"

Cheesy, but guys would either feel bad and want to help, or salivate at the chance to be the first at something. Not only did it help with money, but this technique could also be used on the stage when you were trying to adjust to a new floor, or a new pole, perhaps a new DJ and their music style, and then there were the just plain awkward moments.

We had been making a decent amount of money for a while, well past the ability to use "hi, I'm new here". Here they still had the customers coming in, and when they did they would actually spend money. The downfall to that was it was much more work, as there were not as many Champaign rooms being bought and it required a lot more hustling, but we were leaving with good money in a time when the fancy club wasn't pulling in the clientele with the same cash to blow through.

The club may have been in a location that was not so desirable. After all, we did have a parking lot attendant who watched the cars all night and made sure only customers parked in the lot. Then there was the DJ, who wouldn't play certain types of music, hoping to keep the aesthetic of the club a little bit more upscale than the dingy, vandalized, sketchy, neighborhood we were situated in.

I was happy with how the night had been going, I had made a decent amount of money in private dances as well as on the stage. The club was starting to get busier even though it was getting later. I was surprised they had let people in as late as they did, but if they wanted to pay the cover knowing the cub had to close at a certain time, then the club would gladly accept the money.

I was trying to thread my way through the crowd of people, seeing if anyone wanted a dance. It was useless though. This late in the night, the crowd was not about spending money. Not only that, the customers were younger groups of people, with an unusual amount of ladies, all who were out to have a good time at a local club that also happened to have naked girls.

When it was like this, I didn't waste my time asking anyone for anything walking around the stage. I knew that I would make good money once I was on top of the stage though.

For some reason it seemed that the younger crowds of men and women were less apt to spend money on a private dance but would throw it down on the stage. Luckily for me, I liked working the stage rather than trying to coax a dance or a room.

I went to the bar and grabbed a Shirley temple; this way it looked like it was a drink but was non-alcoholic. I sat at the bar sipping my drink waiting for my set to get called.

I watched the customers around me rather than the girls on the stage. People laughing, groups talking. I was glad they checked for weapons at the door, because there were a lot of people and they had to be people who lived in the area if they weren't spending any money this late. Being in the city, there was bound to be people who didn't get along.

When the customer base started to tip to being an equal amount of men and women, not only would the money dwindle for dances but the energy shifted. Testosterone raged and tempers riled easier as the feeling of a night club started to waft over the crowd rather than that of a strip club.

The song was about to end. I set my drink down on the bar top and hopped off my stool. I gave my thigh highs a tug bringing them up to just under the lip of my ass before reaching for my drink. With my glass in hand I set out across the floor towards the stage.

I started up the short flight of stairs that would take me to the height of the stage. I waited on the side as the girl collected her money. It didn't take her very long as she had kept a close eye on most of it while she danced. Grabbing her clothes she walked over towards me.

"Good luck girl. They wouldn't keep their hands to themselves. And watch out for the group on the end, they'll grab the money and reuse it if they can."

"Thanks for the heads up" I said to her.

Most of the girls didn't waste their time telling you things like that, but I had helped her with her shoes one night when she was pretty drunk and apparently she didn't forget it. I honestly didn't think she would even remember, but the tip she just shared made me think she did.

"I'm fucking tired and over this shit tonight." She went on, "my man is coming to get me, he's gonna be pissed that I didn't make any money but how can I with this fucking crowd. Hopefully you make some money on this last set. I'm gonna try to grab one more dance before I head up."

"Good luck" I replied. She was already teetering off to the corner she had her eye on.

I turned towards the crowd and took a deep breath. Let's do this I thought as I made my way towards the pole. I couldn't do much more that twirl around it, and wouldn't try more than that with a crowd like this. I was practicing climbing the pole, but hadn't done anything more than look like a baby bear trying to climb a sapling looking for honey in a beehive hanging up high.

I grabbed the pole with one hand and began to walk around it, putting one healed foot down in front of the other, almost like a flamingo. I hadn't even gotten around the pole one time when I heard the commotion start.

There is something about a physical fight that you can hear the movements of the body and know something is happening without hearing any actual words. Even with the music thrumming from the speakers, there was an unmistakable noise unlike any other coming from within. I whirled around and sure enough there it was.

In between the bar and the stage was a commotion between two groups of customers. I couldn't tell how many were fighting, if it was just a one on one fight or actual groups of people. As the sound caught up with the sight in front of me, other patrons and dancers started to notice what was happening.

The throng of the crowd had been so thick that the fight almost went unnoticed for a minute. Long enough for something bad to happen I thought to myself. Even being on the stage I still couldn't see what was happening on the floor in front of me. As the volume increased around me, I made my way to the pole. I grabbed it tight with both hands and haphazardly climbed up a few feet.

Just enough to gain a birds eye view, but not enough to fall down and hurt myself. That's all that was needed to go along with the brawl that was ensuing below.

As I was clambering for a higher view the security team realized what was happening and started to charge forward, like a wedge being driven through a tough piece of wood.

I watched, enthralled by the melee of bodies in the mix. From what I could see there were at least three or four people fighting, one of them being one of the girls in the crowd. She was as big as the men fighting, and was holding her own against her challenger.

Try as I might, I couldn't see much in the dim lit interior. Security had made there way to the center of the incident and was holding the sparring parties apart. I watched as they collected them and all but dragged them out.

Below me there were knocked over chairs and girls in hysterics. I was clinging to my perch watching as the remaining crowd started to pick up the chairs and righten themselves. It was near closing time, but everyone inside seemed more comfortable hanging out for a minute knowing all of the fighting parties were now just outside the door.

I scanned the room for my friend, eager to see where she was and if she was ok. I didn't doubt her safety, but was curious if she had witnessed the minor buzz of activity. It would at least add some excitement to the ride home I thought. I gingerly slid down the pole, careful about my bare skin sticking on my thighs, squeaking despite the care.

There was a buzz of excitement all around me. The remaining customers who were there to spend money had gathered their things and headed out. The nights activities had been just a bit much for them. The remaining locals were talking to each other. The DJ had ended for the night, so the music wasn't on anymore. The lights came on, and that was my cue to grab my stuff and head upstairs. I quickly gathered my clothes and money and headed to the edge of the stage. I wasn't in the mood to talk to anyone with the lights on.

It was like a hearty dose of reality with the lights on. My stage persona meeting the real me, and the two worlds didn't mix well. I maneuvered around the excess of bodies and got into the stairwell without incident. The people there weren't paying attention to the dancers, so it wasn't the same as a regular night and I wasn't complaining.

By the time I hit the stairs I took a deep breath and headed up the narrow passage way. I fucking hated climbing the stairs in my heels after walking around in them all night. My feet were sore and my muscles were screaming at me. I hit the top landing and sighed out loud as I walked into the dressing room.

The room was buzzing from the girls talking about the fight.

"two gangs"

"local kids"

"girl whooped his ass"

"chair thrown"

"fighting outside"

I heard snippets from everyone talking. Some of the girls were on their phones so it was a one sided conversation, and others were chit chatting while they changed. By the time I had gotten to my bag my feet felt like they were on fire and I was sure I was limping.

My friend was just taking her shoes off, so I had time to sit and take a breath.

"Holy shit, did you see that?" I said, joining into the gossip around me.

"A little" she said "I was coming out of my private when security was rushing over to them. By the time I got to the stairs they were dragging them out"

"I climbed the pole" I said laughing. "I couldn't see, but it was right there when I was on the stage so I hopped up to try to watch. And I figured I would be out of the way of anything flying."

"My feet are killing me" I said as I undid the strap around my ankle on the first shoe. "I cannot wait to take these off and put my sandals on." I rubbed the ball of my left foot, before I started taking off the second shoe.

There was nothing like the comfort of putting on a pair of flat shoes after a night of dancing in heels. Even though these had a great cushion in them, there is nothing that helps hours of dancing in heels night after night. The second most comfortable thing was taking off the g-string and the thigh highs and putting on sweat pants and a t-shirt. Pure bliss.

Creature of the Night

When I was younger I remember watching this movie about a girl who ended up stripping to pay her way through college and raise her child. The one line I remember the most from that movie is "Make the money. Don't let the money make you."

That line stayed in my head during the time that I danced. Every night that I went into work there are choices that must be made. Working in the seedy underbelly of society, a girl sees things. There are offers of sex, drugs, and your morals and ethics are constantly questioned. Everything has a price, and you have to decide how far you are willing to go in order to make the money you need.

Me, I just needed to pay my bills. I didn't have an abusive controlling boyfriend who collected my money at the end of the night. I didn't have a raging drug addiction that I had to feed while also trying to make enough money to pay my rent.

More importantly, I didn't develop either of these as I spent more and more time around them. When offers of cocaine and molly were presented in turn for a dance or as a benefit of a private room I declined. After that I would see the same guy take another girl in the back and I knew she didn't decline the offer.

Sure enough they would come out later and both of them had the look of getting high.

I might miss the opportunity to make some money, but I was saving who I was on the inside. I was making money, the money was not going to make me.

There are some things that just cannot be avoided though. Sleep and the flip into a creature of the night are inevitable even though I tried to maintain secrecy of what we were doing. Eventually the late nights and early mornings couldn't be hidden. I was showing up bleary eyed and yawning almost every Friday and Monday.

I was passing off the sleepless behavior on an actual second job at a local factory that I had gotten at the start of the summer. I had started working their to make ends meet, having recently separated from my daughters father. The shifts worked were the night shifts, so the transition from working there versus working in the club was smooth.   There was a little difference on the time that we left and the time that we got home, but I just told the babysitter, who also happened to be my mother, that I was going in early to try to get some overtime.

The lack of sleep was something that I could get away with, but there are other little changes that come along with working the night. The clothes worn, the attitude, the shift in proper behavior in society that doesn't come off like you are a stripper.

There is something about walking around in heels and lingerie, dancing naked or next to naked on a stage, asking for private dances and champagne rooms while trying to make as much money as possible, that loosens your sensibilities and relaxes the mundane.

If we were going out for a night on the town heels and a barely there outfit were proper. I mean, when you spend most of the time naked, a dress is a step up and certainly covering the assets completely is acceptable.

Sweatpants became the normal outfit, along with any shoe that was not a heel. The best feeling was to sit down after a long night, lean over and loosen the tight straps that ran along my ankle. Pulling the strap back in on itself, removing its bond with my skin and peeling each foot out of its self imposed torture device

Once the binds were removed and the shoes sat lifeless in a pile on the floor, peeling down the restrictive pieces of clothing that felt like ropes held tight was refreshing. Sitting in the chair, a shirt draped over the seat to know what I let my bare flesh sit upon, rolling my ankles and pulling out the coziest piece of clothing. My favorite sweatpants.

There is no better feeling than warm cozy clothing after walking around in next to nothing for hours on end.

We spent so much time dolled up at work, then when we weren't headed into the club we tended to do nothing with ourselves. My hair would just get thrown up in an elastic, and I didn't bother with something as simple as mascara.

My friend started to get very deep into the mentality of everything has a price, and would show that side when we were even going out for fun.

"Are you going to give me money to talk to me? No? Ok then, get away from me" was something I would frequently hear from her when we went out to the bar and some guy tried to talk to her.

See when everything you do out at a regular nightclub can earn you money at a strip club, why keep doing it for free. When the body, the conversation, the whole 'being' of a woman, is monetized, the psyche starts to shift. As if money isn't something that everyone thinks about regularly, it turns into something even more consuming.

It becomes harder to look at men the same once you have seen them take the mask off. After nights repeated of hearing them speak freely, listening to the things that they hold back from saying when in society, it becomes harder to treat men the same. The first time an old man who looked like the friendly grandfather spewed some lewd remarks about what he wanted to do with me, I was shocked and mortified.

Call me naive, but I was not ready to have a Jolly Saint Nick, think back to the movie Ernest Saves Christmas, talk about my ass or my vagina. As he threw money and kept up the conversation, it was hard to not feel appalled. I kept my thoughts to myself, obviously, but from that moment on I could never look at an old man as innocent as I did before.

You see a side of people that you don't expect to see, especially because when people pay for things they think they own them. Almost like a boss at a regular company who pays an hourly wage so they can put any task on your plate, but without the HR department to worry about.

The underbelly of society is a dark place where people undo the tightly glued mask and let you see them for who they are. The odd requests, the vulgar talk, the ownership of another person with the enticement of money. Its a service exchanged, they pay you and you do not judge while providing some of their inner desires.

The Foot Fetish

I was walking around the club for a little while and had yet to make any real good money. It was pretty busy and I knew I could make more than the six hundred that I had wrapped around my wrist.

The club circuit wasn't to bad because there were lots of people coming in and out tonight. I stopped at a table with two younger guys at it, they had just gotten a couple of drinks as their cups were still full.

"Hi guys How are you tonight?" I smiled at them as I stopped near the edge of the table.

"Hi" the one closest to me said. "We just got here." He was being polite but didn't really want to talk to me. The other guy with him just looked out, not making eye contact.

I smiled at them, they thought I was going to ask if they wanted a dance right away and this was the subtle art of how to tell me they didn't want to engage; hopefully, it was not just yet and not for the whole night.

The thing about a strip club is that all men are looked at like prey when they walk in. On a slow night a guy can have proposals from five girls before he's even got his drink, all vying to get his money. It can get tedious for the customers who are looking to spend just a little bit of money and enjoy the vibe. On the other end, they came to a place that is literally all about spending money.

"Its a little busy tonight, I've been walking around a lot. Do you mind if I just pause here with you for a minute and give my feet a rest?" I smiled innocently at them. This would either hit or miss. They would engage in conversation or be pissed that I was talking to them. Depending on how they acted would determine if I would actually stay and talk to them.

"Ehh, whatever" replied the one who didn't make eye contact.

Smiling at them, I ignored the sullen tone and tried to strike up a conversation. "Are you guys from around here" I started, simple ice breaker.

"No."

"Oh, do you come here often?"I asked

"Sometimes"

"Do you usually come on Sunday nights?" I tried again.

"No."

"You guys gonna be here for long tonight?" Last attempt.

"Maybe."

"Oh, well, I wont keep you guys I can tell you're not much for conversation. Thanks for the rest and have a good night." I smiled at them as I replied my exit, not waiting to hear the next monotone reply.

I sashayed off to start working again. At least I had given my feet a brief break; when standing I could shift from one foot to the other and relieve some of the pain in each foot one at a time.

The next group was not far away, only this time they were a bit older. There really was a huge difference between the ages of men and how they acted. It was harder to get the younger guys to spend money, as they had this attitude of they weren't going to pay for something they could get for free. They were more apt to ask you to an afterparty rather than a dance, but they weren't as lewd. The older, middle aged guys would spend money a hell of a lot easier but they were more apt to try and touch you or ask for their dollar to be spent on things I wasn't offering.

I walked up to the small group who were standing away from any of the tables.

"Hi Guys!" I smiled cheerfully at them. "How are you tonight?" I rested my hand on the shoulder of the guy closest to me, alerting him to my intrusion on their conversation.

"Hi" They all amicably replied to me.

"Well aren't you a pretty little thing" The one across from where I was standing said, as he appraised me up and down.

And that was another difference between the older and younger crowds. The older men were not abashed at telling you exactly what they thought.

"Why thank you." I replied coyly, smiling at him and dropping my eyes a little bit. We could both dance to the beat of the game tonight.

"Are you looking to get any dances tonight" I said to him, a devilish glean in my eye, as I lifted one corner of my mouth in a sultry, wanna play kind of way.

"For you, I think I might be" guy across from me replied again.

"Do you want to go now, or do you have to get to know me first?" Another coy smile at him. I was goading him just a little bit, implying that he would have to get to know me before putting out. Kind of like how men do to women, and so I was questioning his virility.

His friends laughed, which is what I was hoping for.

"I'm ready for you" He said.

"All right then, lets go" I walked over to him, taking his arm into mine as if we were a couple about to head out from dinner.

His circle was cat-calling him as we started off, I could hear the comments fading as we stepped out of the circle and became engulfed with the sounds coming from the DJ booth.

"You're beautiful" he said to me. "What's your name?"

" Mallory" I said smiling, "and thank you. What's your name? I asked him in return.

"Allen. I haven't seen you here before, do you usually work here?"

"I only come here one night a week, but I also do Saturday mornings sometimes. I usually work at the other clubs that they have."

"I've been to one of the others, but not the junior one."

"Oh, thats the one I'm usually at."

Our friendly conversation continued as we made our way across the club and over to the room on the side.

The private dance room here was pretty large compared to others, but was still a small room compared to the club size. In it, there were large cushioned chairs that lined the room with about a foot, maybe two feet of space in between each one. Each chair had its own little table next to it so drinks were not on the floor. It also gave the dancers a place to put their clothes if needed.

The very back of the room had couches, well, small love seats that could comfortably fit two people. These were usually the first to fill up, as they provided a bit more space. Sometimes you would see double dances here, or just a guy and a girl sitting there talking. You could not lay down on them, they were strictly for sitting.

This room also had a large burly security guard who stood nearby, albeit discreetly.

Although the customers didn't like him standing there, as he enforced the house rules such as no touching the dancers. Ironically some of the girls didn't like him standing there either; they said he had a free show, but really it's because they counted on breaking the rules to make some money.

This club was fancier, and all nude. We could, and were expected to, remove all of our clothing both on stage and in the private rooms. I was thankful that there was someone who made sure I wasn't touched or the customers didn't try to do anything I didn't like.

We walked over the threshold and paused, I noticed that the back of the room was empty, with only about four other people in various places throughout the room. I was holding his arm, hanging on him like a good trophy would.

"Where do you want to go?" I asked him, pausing for only a moment, "the back of the room is empty."

"Ya, thats a good spot" he replied. His response was a clue that he may have been here before.

The back of the room was dark and had little interruptions. I knew he would want to go there. We started to cross the room, heading to our own spot. We were lucky to be able to grab one of the love seats in the back, it was usually the first place everyone went, someone else must have just left I figured.

I didn't have to tell him what to do, he sat down and put his drink down on our little table like he had done this before. A seasoned patron.

If they were relatively sober, I would usually wait until a new song came on before I starting. As they paid by the song, if I started in the middle of one they would say that they didn't get a full song that way they didn't feel cheated and I wasn't working longer than I had to. A sober customer would say something to you, at least the regular visitors would.

This guy was both sober and a regular. The song was one I was familiar with, so I knew there wasn't much time left before the next song started. Not only that, the clubs had shortened versions of every song so we would only dance for about three minutes. A song could play on the radio in the car and you feel like it goes on for four to five minutes, but get in the private room of a strip club and that song cuts off real quick!

He was lounging in the corner of the love seat, and I needed room to put both of my legs on either side of him so I could straddle him during the song.

I set my drink down on the small table next to his. The tables were set a little behind the love seat, it made it easy to forget your drink and harder for anyone to tamper with them while you were dancing.

I smiled at him as I moved back in front of him, standing above him and smiling. I leaned down, holding my hair back with my right hand while I braced myself on the arm of the love seat with my left, and moved in closer to him. I needed to be heard over the music

"I'm just waiting for the song to end, its almost over. But can you slide over to the right just a little?" I asked in a sweetly voice, "I'll need just a little bit of room for my legs." I said, still smiling at him standing back up as quick as I had asked

"Oh, ya". And he shuffled himself over a smidge. He readjusted his pants.

I stood in front of him, my heels helped to provide a nice silhouette for him in the dimly lit room. I made sure to keep my body angled in a sexy, seductive manner for him. I lifted both my arms up and placed my hands at the nape of my neck, poised to lift my hair up. Not only did it look good, but it helped give some cool air to a sweaty spot.

My hair was long enough to cascade down, and when it did it felt great. I could feel the sweat at the nape of my neck with my hands now. I picked my hair up and started moving my hips in time with the song that was coming to an end. Slow movements to the ending song was a good segue into the next song that I would dance to. "Our" song started and I moved into my number.

Money hadn't been discussed or exchanged yet. I was thinking of the details that added up to what could be a nice addition of money.

Older.

Repeat customer.

Picked a spot on his own.

Nice clothes, wearing a watch.

What I would do is one song, and then ask if he wanted more. The fact he hadn't paid me up front would mean he wanted to see if he liked my dancing and would then decide if he wanted to pay to spend more time with me.

They didn't all spend the same way, but they all fit into different categories.

The one who comes in wanting a variety so he gets one dance with a bunch of girls, all of which have been decided upon just by looking at them on stage.

The one who has a favorite girl and will only spend on her. This can be from both a possessive girl who dominates him when he's there, or a guy who doesn't like anyone else and only comes for her. He may spend a little bit when his favorite isn't working - but him being there when she isn't working is rare.

And then the one who was like mine, where he will judge the girl only after one dance. If that dance is something he liked then he will spend more money with you. He is usually a one night stand kind of guy. The next time he comes in, he may see you again and he may not.

What that meant for me is that I needed to give him a great dance this time, but not so much that he didn't want to keep going. I was listening to the beat and thinking how I would make sure to leave my thongs on.

I had done most of my little number, and was back to standing so that I could see him. I watched him sweep the room with his eyes. The song was starting to wrap up, he could tell it was almost over also, as his attention came to rest fully on me. I was starting to move in closer to talk money when I heard him say "why don't you just sit next to me for a minute" as he patted the spot next to him on the loveseat.

I felt myself cock my head to the side, much like a little puppy would do when they don't quite understand what was said. Sure I hear him, but it took a second for it to register.

"Oh, ok, if you want." I was going to straddle his lap and ask if he wanted another dance, but I hadn't ever been asked to sit next to someone.

I sat down slowly, which was truthfully a welcome rest for my feet. As I did so, he pulled my legs over to him.

"Is this ok?" He asked of me, as now that I was sitting my legs were straight across his lap.

"Ya thats fine. I don't think they'll say anything about that." It wasn't my ass or tits, so security shouldn't make a big fuss over it. I hoped.

He leaned over towards me, and this was where the deal was struck.

"I owe you twenty for the dance, but how about I give you another eighty, so one hundred in total, to rub your feet and calves for the next song."

I sat there, dumbfounded for a moment. I think my mouth must have been hanging open. I had never been offered money to sit and let someone rub my feet and calves. I mean, I was going to say yes. Who would possibly say no?

"Oh, ok, that sounds ok to me" I felt like I stuttered out.

He shifted and reached behind him to pull his wallet out of his pants. I saw him take out one bill from a wallet that was far from thin. He slid his wallet back into his pants, and then handed me the bill.

"Thank you" I said, smiling, taking the bill and sliding it into the strap of my thong.

"Now" he said "lets take these shoes off of you so I can rub your feet for you". He reach over and started unbuckling the closest shoe while I worked on the other. He slid my shoe off and handed it to me. I took my other one and set them on the floor. I readjusted how I was sitting, making sure that both feet were comfortably in his lap.

He started rubbing both feet, one with each hand. I had given him the ok to rub my calves, and so he was running his hands from my toes up to the nape of my knee. I sighed in pleasure, because this was amazing. I glanced over to the security guard and saw him just shaking his head.

He wouldn't be a problem.

For the next 3 minutes I sat there in bliss as this strange man rubbed my feet and lower calves through my stockings. Never mind the fact that I had just made another eighty dollars for sitting here and enjoying it. If this were a thing, I could certainly get used to it I thought.

Making New Friends

When I had started dancing I pretty much assumed I would be throwing my dating life away. I was newly single, getting ready to go through a divorce and had a toddler at home. WHO would want to date all of that, and now add on that I took my clothes off for men and got paid for it to the mix. Yeah, I thought, my chances are pretty low to find a decent man. But that was ok.

My friend always seemed to meet new people, or had some guy that was coming to see her. We could be at the lake swimming on a hot day while the kids were in school and some guy would show up to hang out with us. We were two beautiful young girls, of course they would want to hang out.

She had met some new guy who also happened to be local, living in the same town. He had told her that he could get weed for her, and that was the in he needed to pass off his number. Soon enough she was calling him for bud when her regular guy didn't give her any.

Jamie showed up for the first time, his friend waiting out in the car. He and my friend did the back and forth that seemed more like a mating dance rather than a sales call. Before I knew it, he was out the door and we were rolling up.

"He gave me a really good deal on this. Let's see how it is." She said to me, sauntering into her bedroom.

All of the kids were gone for the weekend, spending time at their respective fathers. My daughter was gone, and so were her kids. We had the whole weekend to ourselves. Apart from work, we could just enjoy the time.

"Lets go out tonight" she said. "We'll just go out for a drink and play a little bit of pool at the bar up the road from me."

"I'm good with that."

"Jeans, t-shirt, nothing special. I don't even know if I'll do my makeup. Well, I have to do mascara because I don't have any fucking eye lashes. But other than that no makeup."

"When do you want to leave?" I asked.

"I just want to get something clean on, lets finish smoking this." She paused "and then we'll get something to eat before we go drinking."

"That sounds even better." I laughed.

Later that night we were at the local bar playing pool. It was slow for the night of the week, but we weren't complaining. The music was good, the drinks cheap and strong, and we were having a great time. Neither one of us were actually any good at playing pool, although we both acted as if we knew what we were doing it was clear once we hit the ball that we didn't.

It was my turn, and I was leaning over the table lining up my shot for the corner pocket. I felt confident in the shot, but when I let the cue fly it bounced off the white ball, sending it pitifully towards the left of the table. I laughed, standing up shaking my head at the wayward shot.

"Its your turn" I yelled over to her.

"Already" she laughed. "I'm going to go get a refill" she said, "want to come with me? I think I saw Jamies friend come in and I want to see if he'll buy us a drink."

"Ya, I guess."

We made our way over to the corner of the bar, where a couple of guys sat on the stools. I lingered behind her, not really comfortable to approach this friend of a friend. I was gonna let her do all the talking, which is how we usually ended up with free shots or drinks. Whenever a guy would buy her a drink she would ask for two, one for her and one for me. They didn't want to say no to her, so they would buy both drinks.

I didn't mind being the awkward turtle who stood behind the outgoing loud girl who was seemingly without embarrassment. Standing where I was it was hard to hear the conversation, so I was a little surprised when my friend handed me half a shot. I grabbed it, and the question must have shown on my face.

"He didn't want to buy you a shot, so I drank half and you can have the other half."

I made to hand it back to her, "Oh, thats ok. I don't need the other drink."

"Shut up and drink it" she said to me.

I followed her directive, as it was easier to just drink it and not make a scene. I didnt forget his unwillingness to buy two shots instead of one however.

She thanked him and ended the conversation and we went back over to finish our game. We played for a little while longer and I saw Jamie's friend, I hadn't even gotten his name which was fine with me, head on out the door.

"He's leaving" I said "What a dick. I didn't need the shot, but I've never met anyone who blatantly said no before."

"Ya, he's a weird one but fuck him." She said.

I hoped I wouldn't see him again, but if he was friends with Jamie then it was likely I wouldn't get my wish. We finished up our game and decided to head home for the night.

When you spend enough time out in bars and clubs they lose their appeal and you start to see the grungy dirty side to them. Pool hall or strip club, they are all part of the underbelly of society. They just weren't as much fun once you see behind the scenes.

We started the walk back to her house, which wasn't far. It was late, but there was no worry about walking home alone. Even though there were dark places along the route, we had both grown up in the area and knew that the likelihood of something happening was slim to none. There are advantages to living in a small town. Besides, there were two of us and we were both ferocious in our own rights.

I sighed as we walked, thinking about the two encounters during the day, Jamie and his strange friend at the bar. Jamie was nice enough, although he likely wanted something from my friend. His friend, whatever his name was, was another story. How people become friends always amazed me, especially when they seemed to be opposites. I had a feeling we would be seeing a lot more of the two of them.

Come see me at work

We were back at the smaller sister Club that was in a more restrictive, run down part of town. Although the rules didn't allow it to be so revealing here, the money was good here.

We had heard that the upscale club had died down a little bit. It made sense, as that club was more money to get in and the girls themselves were a little higher end. Dances cost more money, private rooms cost more money, even the drinks cost more money. We may have been at a smaller club that was on the unsavory part of town, but right now we were making more money.

The type of clientele that we were seeing were used to the hard economic times, whereas the clientele that went to the upscale club weren't as quick to spend their money lately.

Even still, the night was slow. There are only so many laps around the club floor that you can walk before you get tired of just walking, seeing the same faces.

I had been talking to this guy for a little while, and he knew where I was working. We met through a friend, his friend happened to know my friend. Classic way to meet people, and it made it easy to talk to guys who got along. The four of us would go out together.

It was slow, so I walked back to the dressing room so I could text him. It was like my feet knew where I was and started to ache as soon as I got through the door. I limped over to my stuff and sat in the chair.

I kept my phone on me, in my little clutch. I pulled it out and found his text thread in my messages.

"You should come see me tonight. Its sooo slow." I sent him, smiling to myself. If I couldn't make money at least I could pass the time with someone who I liked.

But it was more than that. This guy knew I was dancing, but he hadn't seen that side of me. That sexy, seductress side. We had only went out a few times to the local bar, which meant jeans and a top with some low key makeup. There was a part of me that wanted him to see the stage performer.

It felt empowering, a rush of dopamine that stemmed from desire. It was intoxicating.

I sat for another minute, letting my feet rest. I heard the familiar ding of the alert letting me know that I had a new message.

"We're on our way. Send us the name."

I felt like my breathing stopped and suddenly I felt like a nervous school girl with my first crush.

Shit. What had I done. I mean, sure I wanted to see him, but then again I did not want to see him. Gah...

To late now. I sighed to myself, and sent him the name.

We had about 45 minutes to an hour before they showed up at a minimum. Better go tell my friend that they were coming. Her night had seemed just as slow as mine, so she would hopefully enjoy the distraction.

I wasn't that far off with my assumption, I found. After walking the club a few times I was able to find her.

"What time do you think they'll be here?" She asked.

"Well, they probably didn't leave right away." I thought out loud. I paused, working the timeline in my head from when he answered me, to how long it would take for them to get to the club.

"We have an hour still, if not more." I started, "they probably will stay until closing time, as its already eleven thirty."

And so the wait began until they arrived.

I saw them walk in the door. They had to stop at the bouncer just inside the entrance to have their IDs checked. They were new faces, but the city we were in was big enough that they blended in seamlessly with all the other patrons. Not the splash they would have made at one of our other clubs on such a slow night.

My heart was racing. I had garnered a couple other private dances while I had been waiting for them to show up, and with no other new customers I wasn't going to miss out on any money while they were here; but likewise, none of the customers would be looking for me.

Now, one might wonder why on earth would I willingly have this man that I was talking to come to a club where I danced for other men with my clothes off for money.

The only logic I have to this is the power that I felt on the stage, as a beautiful naked female form where the attention is on you. That moment when you look in a mans eyes and what stares back at you is nothing but carnal lust and desire. Where in that moment they want nothing other than to eat you alive. There is something even more powerful to it when you can go home with them.

I didn't sleep with my customers. I didn't cross the line from visual entertainment to physical entertainment. Anytime the customers looked at me this way, which meant I was doing my job, it either fueled the seductress inside of me or made me think of the money they would give me.

So, I had this guy I was sleeping with come see me.

It was awkward when they first got to the club, because his friend who was sleeping with my friend had never seen me in a bathing suit let alone platform shoes with thongs and fishnets. Likewise, the guy I was sleeping with was now looking at my friend in her stripper outfit.

There are some things that just start to not matter when you dance naked for money. The way in which women carry themselves changes. Their modesty changes. If they have anything on that is more than underwear, then that is more than what they wear to work.

That first bit of uncomfortableness wore off rather quickly, once the boys settled in. We were after all, just at work. We sat with them at the bar for a little bit, they looked like every other customer that came in to the club. Just two friends who were stopping in for a drink.

They bought us each a drink and we sat on opposite sides of them, talking for a little bit.

Finally I smiled, and with a mischievous grin leaned over closer to his ear and asked him

"Wanna go for a dance?" Giggling as I did so.

I leaned back, and he saw the smile on my face.

"Alright" he said, "lets go."

He grabbed his drink, and made to stand up. I had to wait for him to move off the chair because we had been sitting so close.

When he was up, I started the process of lifting one cheek off the stool slowly, as not having full cover on my ass I was sticking.

Finally up with both heels on the ground, I turned and grabbed my drink. By this time my friend was looking at me wondering where we were going.

"Gonna head to the back" I mouthed to her.

He didn't know where we were going, so when I turned to him I looped my arm through his as if he were leading me throughout a ballroom with both of us in finery. When I started walking he had no choice but to walk with me, and like this, I led him over to the private dance area.

What I didn't think about was how nervous I was going to be. I did this same walk, this same performance night after night, yet for some reason I felt like it was my first time. My legs were shaking as I walked across the club with him. I breathed in deep and told myself to cut the shit. I took a deep breathe, a sip of the tequila I had in my cup, and tried to set myself onto auto pilot.

I sat him down in the corner of the room, setting my drink down on the table next to him. I realized two things in that moment. The first was that if I gave him to good of a dance, he might think that I do that for everyone. The second was that if I gave him too bad of a dance, he would wonder why he drove all this way and what was I doing to make money.

It was a conundrum I hadn't thought about. I didn't have long before a decision had to be made on what the next steps were going to be. I decided that I was going to play the tease route, and not really touch him very much. I would dance standing up, while he just watched. Then if he asked me to come closer, I would.

This plan was working, I danced for most of the entire song without touching him. He looked at me, and motioned for me to come closer. I took the cue and sat on his lap. I told him to just keep his hands on the arm rests.

"I can sit here, you just can't touch me. It doesn't seem like it, but the DJ is watching in the mirrors." I said.

I leaned in closer to him

"I'm glad you came up here tonight." I said to him. I didn't wait to hear what he said, and instead started to dance on him for the rest of the song.

It didn't last very long, which I had known would happen. The songs never lasted quite as long as the regular versions, and this song was played routinely so I had a goof gauge on when it would be finishing. I stood up, having never taken any of my clothes off, there was nothing to put on so I moved a little quicker than normal.

"You ready to head back?" I asked him, smiling at him. With my heels on, I was looking down on him. He had a slightly glazed look on his face, as if the lights had just turned on and surprised him. I gave him a couple seconds to compose himself, coming back to the present. He reached for his drink, and we began to make our way back to the bar.

"Perfect timing!" Exclaimed my friend was rounding the edge near the dance area just as we started to walk out of it.

"This customer wants a private room, the two of us!" She said discreetly to me, our heads leaned in towards each other.

"What?!" I replied, a little to harsh. "He wants me to come with you?" I was shocked at the proposal, only because in all the time we had worked together we had never went into a private room with a customer. Sure we had done a couple little stage interactions, but never anything that was one on one with someone in private.

"He said he has been in here before and he has been thinking about the two of us together ever since. He said its both of us or none of us, and he is willing to pay the double fee for the room." She all but squeaked out. "We haven't made any money, and I know that they are here but we need this." She went on.

I knew she wasn't wrong.

"Ok let me just tell him." I said to her.

We had stopped right outside of the private dance area to talk, and by this time he had come up behind me. I turned to him to tell him I had to go back to work.

"So this customer wants a double champagne room." I nonchalantly said. "He asked for the two of us, and we haven't really made that much money so I am not going to pass it up tonight. It will only be for a half hour, so it won't be the whole night."

It was dark in the area we were in, so I wasn't able to see the contours and whether or not he was angry. It didn't really matter anyways, he knew where I was.

"I'll see you in a little bit" I said to him.

Off we went to the bar, where I could see the customer standing next to the bartender.

"I grabbed you a dirty Shirley to drink" my friend said to me as we linked arms and sauntered to the bar "the room comes with a free drink for us."

I was going to need it.

Saturday Afternoon

I had always thought that a strip club was only open at night. Call my naive, but it just seemed to go hand in hand with activities that happened at night. That thought was quickly dashed when we got scheduled to work at the upscale club for Saturday day shift.

"Shift starts at noon, doors open at ten-thirty for you to come in and get ready." The house mom has told us as we planned our schedule.

I know my face displayed the shock, I don't really have a poker face after all. The house mom had chuckled.

"I know it's early," she said, "but we get a lot of business men who come in around lunch time. It will be a good shift for you both. You're gonna work from noon to six and the house fee is reduced so you will only have to pay forty dollars for the day."

"Ohhh, that makes sense. Ok, Saturday it is."

And Saturday it was. We were arriving for our first shift during the day and it felt weird. If you have ever been inside of a club when they turn all the lights on, it is kind of like that. Suddenly the magic of the night is dashed and the blinders are pulled off as you see the shiny veneer get pulled off. That's what it was like arriving in the day.

That disappeared when we walked inside however. The club didn't have any windows, so inside it didn't matter the time of the day. The music was on low and the black lights were on.

We trudged up to the second floor dressing room, both of us tired from the night before. We had left the house at nine am to make the hour and a half ride to the club to arrive for ten thirty so we could have enough time to get ready. The only bonus was we would be done by six pm.

I yawned loudly, not even bothering to mask my tiredness yet. "I just hope the day shift is worth me losing the sleep I could have had" I said.

"Let's get this money. It will be a different clientele during the day. Hopefully these business men spend." My friend said.

We proceeded to get ready as normal. The contrast between it being morning and me applying my nighttime makeup still felt weird, and that was only amplified when I put my outfits on. There's just something about black fishnet stockings that screams black lights and evening activities. I brushed that all aside as I remembered the role that I was here to play.

These men, for thats what made up the majority of patrons, came here for the illusion of fantasy. Whether it be a woman shaking their ass on a stage or a pretty face getting paid for their conversation, they had expectations of how their money would be spent. At least thats what I had experienced up until my first day shift.

I've been in a bar during the day; as a kid my step-mom would take me to the local watering holes for an afternoon beer every weekend I was with her. Usually the people who go to a bar during the day are there for a drink. While they may not be getting as drunk as on say, Friday night, they are there for the effects brought on by the alcohol.

Strip clubs, although they contain a bar, can be used for a variety of things, but they still usually have the feeling of being a bar. The majority of people come inside and they tend to be creatures of habit. Their first stop is the bar, and then once they have a drink only then will they proceed to sit, or entertain themselves with the company of one of the girls.

Daytime hours however, at least at this club, were different. The clientele that came in were not looking to really drink. Sure, there were a few of the customers who were drinking as soon as the clock turned 12:01, but the majority were purposefully there for the discreet atmosphere or the entertainment.

It was almost as if the club had become an extension of the board room. There were more men in suits or slacks and a blazer than I had ever seen at one time in the club. The night shifts brought out people who were unwinding from work. The day shift brought in people who were at work.

It still felt like a bar, but when the side door would open the sunlight streamed in, shining a light on the dark within. It snapped me back to reality every time someone opened the door.

The customers who were drinking would have one drink during the entirety of their visit. They would sit at the stage, men in their suits drinking their gin and tonics, as they discussed business while putting ten and twenty dollar bills down in front of them.

Their visits were shorter and right to the point. The men were not lingering around, letting hours pass by. Rather they were on lunch breaks, or entertaining out of town business associates and colleagues. Dances were easy to come by, without the hassle of trying to dance around spending time with them.

That first day shift we worked ended up being great. The clients weren't as numerous as the night shift, but when they spent money they really spent money. Although we had gotten there at what felt like the crack of dawn, we were going to be able to leave work when it was still daylight out.

I hadn't seen my friend for most of the shift while we worked, we were on opposite stage sets. It also meant we both had a great day. When I had climbed on stage at the beginning of my set the DJ had announced that it would be the last rotation for us, which meant that it was close to six. I thought I had seen some of the night shift girls coming in, which meant they would be coming down soon for the next stage set.

The day shift had flown by. I climbed down off the stage bar top and started to wind my way through the crowd that was starting to pick up. The night shift girls were starting to make their way down to the main bar. The few that were walking past me were in full ball gowns. Interesting. I hadn't seen that before, but I recalled the house mom telling us that to work on Friday or Saturday night it required a little bit more attention to outfits and makeup.

I was here to make money, and while I had to invest a little in my wardrobe to do that I was not quite willing to drop the coinage needed to spring for the full ball gown and beauty queen makeup. It was one thing to spend sixty dollars with the women who brought in custom made outfits during a shift. It was another to spend hundreds on an outfit that would only be worn one or two nights per week.

Working on a Friday or Saturday night would not only need the expensive outfits, but the house fee would be double what we normally paid. Besides, I wasn't making the money that these girls could make. Perhaps I wasn't good at selling a lie, making promises I wouldn't keep, swindling money, or it's because I was not selling more than a dance. Whatever the reason, my income was not high enough to gain me entry to work on Friday or Saturday nights.

Truthfully, that was okay with me. I knew that I wasn't the prettiest, or had the best body. I didn't have my boobs done, so that took a whole source of revenue off the table for me. I did have a big ass, which even though out brought another set of clients, it was a much smaller margin than those that preferred a big chest.

Saturday day shift had brought me a decent amount of money with a small house fee and I was going to be home for the rest of the night. It wasn't a bad deal.

I was sitting in the dressing room changing into my street clothes. I had sweatpants and a tank top today. As soon as I put it on I morphed back into the girl that would be found at the local Walmart.

The only thing that stood out was the face of dramatic makeup and the straightened hair. Looking in the mirror, my reflection said that I was probably getting ready to go out for the night, not that I had just paraded around the club in lingerie making money for the last size hours.

I sighed to myself, sometimes I wondered what I was even doing here.

Tampon Strings

Periods. Even a dancer can't escape Mother Nature. I was a little more fortunate in the fact that I didn't classify as "regular", so it wasn't such a regular occurrence as the other girls.

But alas, Aunt Flo did come knocking on my door every so often and there was no way to stop her from barging on in.

I watched one of the other girls come out of the bathroom and kick her leg up onto the counter, pulling her panties aside as she looked in the mirror. I tried not to stare, but then I watched her lower her foot, bend over and spread her cheeks as she peered back at herself.

Good thing she was tall I thought, otherwise she wouldn't be able to see over the counter top.

I wasn't sure what she was looking for at first, but then as she stood up she grabbed a pair of scissors off the counter moving to place them inside of her bag.

She must have noticed me looking at her put the small shears away because she laughed as she looked back at me in the mirror.

"Cuttin that rip cord so I can bend over" She told me. "I'm not riskin someone seein it with it just shoved all up in there" She explained.

The revelation of this idea must have shown on my face as I stared back at her.

"That's so smart." I said to her.

"Don't give me the credit, it ain't my idea" She laughed.

Naturally, during my tenure dancing one of my most embarrassing moments would involve a tampon string.

We were working at a club that happened to have two different sides: bottoms on, or bottoms off.

The bottoms on side served alcohol, was only open to those over twenty-one, and closed at the same time a regular bar held as closing times for the state that we were in.

The bottoms off side was the opposite.

This side was eighteen and above and only served juice or non-alcoholic drinks. Because of this, the club could stay open until well past regular bar closing times.

The girls could also go full nude, with their bottoms and tops off.

There was no connection between bars on the inside, as they were considered two separate establishments with two separate entrances. The girls could go back and forth between either side if they wanted, but it involved going outside to get between them.

Not everyone wanted to take their bottoms off either, so not everyone would work the other juice bar side.

As we had been working in a state that made it hard to make money with bottoms on, this wasn't the case for us.

I didn't like to go to the bottoms off side if I didn't have to though. But, I liked to make money, so I wasn't opposed to heading over, if just wasn't going to go rushing over there if I didn't have to.

The night on the twenty one plus side was almost a bust, I had drank a little more than I wanted to and hadn't really made a ton of money due to the lack of customers in the building. The bar was going to have to close within the next hour but my friend didn't want to leave just yet. I wasn't complaining as I wanted to make a little bit more to leave with in my pocket. We decided to take a quick trip over to the other side.

We were going to leave our things in the locker room here, and then quickly run outside. As long as we were fully covered then we could go between the clubs. Once we got inside the bouncers would let us pass right through.

When we got inside there were so many people, I couldn't believe how busy it was compared to the horrible night we had been having next door. I guess I should have paid attention a little better, but the irony of not smoking cigarettes was that I didn't venture outside and so I couldn't see the parking lot.

As we got inside we stopped to talk to the bouncer who was working for the rest of the night. We were in the entrance way where the cover charge would be collected. On the counter behind the register there was a shelf that had the drinks served inside. It was lined with cans of soda, a Powerade, and bottles of water.

They were covered in dust, as if they had been there since the club had opened. "Look at the drinks served" I said, laughing, as I pointed up to the shelf.

"You girls been working next door all night?" He asked us, as if it wasn't obvious with our coats, fishnets, and platform black pleather heels.

"Ya, they're closing and we wanted to get some time in here if we can." My friend said. "Its our first time on this side."

"I thought I saw you next door, but I know you haven't been in her before." He responded, looking at his watch. "Ok, I can put you two on together for one stage set, you have to work at least one. Other than that, private dances are in the back room. There's no alcohol for you or them and they can't touch you. Anyone caught doing anything other than dancing will be asked to leave." He said, looking at both of us as he said all this.

I was a little bit tipsy, so I laughed my response to him "sounds good" we both replied. I couldn't help but continue on "as if we would do anything other than dance."

"I didn't mean you would sweetheart, but we're near a base and just because they're under age doesn't mean they aren't drinking. Listen for your names, you'll probably be up at the end of this song. You can put your coats on the rack behind the bar. Tipping is separate from next door." He said, winking as he walked away towards the DJ booth.

We followed his advice and headed towards the coat rack that was behind the bar. Once we had hung them up we turned and assessed the situation.

The place had a bunch of little round tables with a few chairs around each one. There were at least a dozen or so little tables, and each of them was packed with patrons. It was apparent they were mostly underage; they looked like they had just started growing facial hair. They had to be sailors.

But they also were spending money, which was visible by the bills being thrown to the girl dancing on the stage.

We navigated our way around the tables, working our way through the whole club. We passed by the private dance room, which was very different from the side next door. This room was brighter, but at the same time offered more privacy.

Each seat was designed in a half circle, the back reaching high up with a scalloped edge at the top. They reminded me of a clamshell. There was a wave to the pattern they were set in the room, which took advantage of the small space. The room stretched beyond what I could see, and even with the mirrors on the opposing wall I couldn't see all the way to the end.

We didn't have a reason to enter into the room, so we kept it moving past that to continue checking out the club. It was weird to see people drinking cans of soda or bottles of water. Even without the alcohol they were still rowdy, with the boys closest to the stage hooting and hollering at whatever the girl up there was doing.

We wound our way around, careful to not step on anyone. The vibe here was different. They didn't seem up for conversation, at least not with us. The tables that were set back from the stage were talking amongst themselves, laughing at some joke that was told or a recap of their day.

The tables near the stage were focused on the stage. They were throwing money, so if we got up there we would likely bring home something. The private dance room had people in it, so it couldn't be all that bad.

The bar would be the point we would head to after making the circuit around. It was a great place to set up and take it all in without looking like you didn't have anywhere to go. We could at least wait until we were called up to the stage from there.

The wait didn't take long, which did not help my quest to sober up before heading up on stage. We heard the DJ say our names over the loud speaker, and we started to wind our way up towards the three little stairs that were near the DJ booth at the back of the stage.

It didn't take that long to get through the throng of men. It was as if they knew we hadn't worked over here all night and were eager to see what new meat would be put on the stage. They were probably regulars, I thought to myself. Even though we had been working next door, most of the guys couldn't enter because they were under 21. To them, we were the new girls. Hopefully that paid off in our pocket books.

I was nervous to get on stage, and tried to breathe through the increasing anxiety that was sitting in my chest. I had done this at least a hundred times I told myself. There is no reason to be nervous.

But I hadn't been drinking at work for some time and the fear of falling on my face in heels would never go away. Especially on a new stage. We had climbed the stairs and were at the back of the stage while we waited for the girl to grab her money off the floor. She was sweeping it all up, but she had amassed a bit of ones so we waited while she collected them.

If we didn't wait, there was a chance that our money would get mixed in with hers, or vice versa. I took a sip of my drink and set it down at the back of the stage.

As she moved towards the back of the stage, large breasts swaying with her gait as she held her clothes and money tightly to her chest. She would walk right off stage and back to the changing room to collect herself.

We moved towards the front in tandem, my Its Showtime face was quickly replacing the bored look that wouldn't make any money. People - men - came to the club for a fantasy, not a dour faced vision.

The stage was packed, with youthful, hairless faces sitting around the edge. The excitement of fresh bodies was palpable amongst the crowd and they eagerly placed their bills in front of them hoping we would bestow a personal show on them while we were up there.

My friend and I were used to sharing the stage with each other, so we effortlessly moved around, working the crowded front row in tandem. The trick was to work the whole stage, grabbing the money as we went. If one guy placed a dollar, I would scoop all the money from him and the two guys around him, giving the three of them my attention.

While my friend was working one side, I worked the other. We would switch, grabbing money from the opposite side as they replaced the money they had put in front of them.

I was working the middle section of the stage, not paying attention to what was happening to the sides. The stage routine was usually the same, but if they put more money out they got a better show. The guys in front of me had put larger bills out, making the work and effort worth it. A twenty earned on stage was made easier than a twenty earned during a private dance.

At least on the stage there weren't hands trying to touch you. It was clear to the bouncers watching if they did and then at least it would be stopped.

I was laying on the stage on my back, my legs straight in the air as I leaned on my elbows. I was windmilling my legs around, bending at the knees and then splaying my legs wide; a classic stripper move that allowed me to catch a quick break from shaking my ass in their faces.

It was a move that was teasing them, giving them a quick look at the sweet spot between my legs. I still had my panties on, but I could move them to the side for the high paying guys in front of me.

I did just that, making eye contact with the kid in front of me. He smiled as I slid them over. I was feeling the music, and was high on the rush of desire felt from the men in the club.

It was while I was looking at him that I noticed a mirror on the structural column next to them. I looked at myself in the mirror, and it was then that I saw it.

A white line against pink flesh.

I looked at the guy in front of me in horror. He had to have seen it, there was no avoiding it and if I saw it in a mirror he had to have seen it.

He smiled up at me. Maybe he hadn't seen it, I thought to myself. Did I get that lucky?? I smiled back at him as if it had never happened. I wasn't going to make it worse than it was.

I quickly closed my legs and kept them that way for the rest of the time we were on stage. I smiled and winked and

Even though I was drunk for most of that stage set, the embarrassment that I felt in that moment is something I would never forget. Ironically, even though I felt embarrassed it did not stop the amount of money that I made on that stage that night.

Not only did we rake in the bills from the drunk sailors, I also landed quite a few private dances.

What had started out as a slow night turned out to be great for what we took home. Even with the double house fees.

The Chiropractor

I was on my usual circuit at the main club, it was a busy night so there were groups of men everywhere. I was walking around, trying to find my next source of money when I stopped at a group of three men who happened to be standing next to the private dance room.

"Hey guys, how are you tonight?" I coyly asked them.

I waited to see how they would receive me, would they be interested or tell me to keep moving.

"Well hi there beautiful, we're good. And how are you doing tonight?" This was from the one closest to me. He was young, but middle aged young.

"I'm good, just getting my steps in walking around this place." I smiled so they would know I was joking with them. "I'm hoping one of you guys would want to get a dance with me?"

There was no point in beating around the bush tonight. It was busy and the men were here for either a good time with the ladies or with their friends.

"Well, my friend just got one but I think we could go for a dance in just a couple of minutes. We were just talking about the week we had and how nice it is to be able to come out tonight and enjoy your company." This was said by the same guy who first talked to me.

It seemed he laid claim to me first, and I was okay with that so long as he spent some money with me.

"Ohh do you all work together or just sharing in each other's misery?" I asked.

Clearly he wanted some conversation before we took off together. Men could be such finicky creatures at times. Some of them did not want to waste time talking, while others needed to talk to you first. I didn't quite get it, as this wasn't a dating game. We were simply going to enjoy what my physical appearance did for them.

Then again, there were those men that came in regularly and bought gifts for the girls. Maybe some of them were in a delusional relationship. I was not trying to offer something that I did not want a part of. I was here to make my money, but I was not going to let the money make me.

"Well, I'm a chiropractor and my friends here all work in different fields. We were comparing some of the doozy requests we've had over the week."

"A chiropractor!" I exclaimed "No way! That's interesting." I laughed "I was always told to stay away from you guys because once you go you will never be able to stop."

He chuckled "I do have a lot of repeat clients. Although they usually do need it for medical reasons."

"What are some of the things that you can fix, or work with?" I politely inquired. He clearly wanted a conversation.

"Well, migraines for one. I work with a ton of people who get migraines and I can help alleviate them."

I stood there and my mouth must have been agape as I replied "No. Way. I have always suffered from migraines and I had no idea that I could go to a chiropractor and have it solved!"

"Its not a cure, but it will stop them for at least a month or two depending on the severity of them."

"I'm in awe" I replied "how do you do that? I get migraines and I didn't know there was anything like this to fix it!" I exclaimed.

"Its a quick adjustment to the neck. I can show you if you want." He said to me.

His friends started laughing, and that was when I realized this was his usual trick to pick up women. I chuckled to myself, because here the only thing he needed was money. Either he didn't want to spend any money, or he was just making conversation.

I didn't care if they were laughing, if this would help with my migraines, I wanted in.

"Yes, show me!" I happily replied to him.

"Ok, I have to work behind you" he said as he started to move behind me.

"Then I'm going to hold onto your head and make a quick movement. When I say relax, just let go." He said to me. I saw him set his drink down on the table behind him as he moved to cradle my head and neck.

"Ok, I'm ready!" I told him

"Ok, this isn't going to hurt but you will hear a pop or crack as I do this."

His hands were warm as I felt him get close behind me. Suddenly I realized why his friends were laughing; this was a way for him to touch me without getting in trouble.

"Now, relax, and 3 - 2 - 1" He counted down.

I listened to him as he had said, let everything go and trust him. Within seconds I heard the crack and felt the release in my neck.

"Oh!" I exclaimed when he was done. "That wasn't to bad, but it was a loud pop!"

He laughed, moving out from behind me. "I usually charge at least a buck twenty five for that same adjustment in my office. Not to bad huh."

I smiled at him "well, I hope it works! So this should alleviate my headaches for awhile then? Thank you so much!"

"125" I said to him, his words dawning on me. "You make more than me!" I laughed. "So, now that I can see what your hands do, want to take me for a dance?" I laughed, smiling at him.

"Do I get it for free after that?" He asked me.

"Oh cut the shit, Bob, take the girl for a dance you didn't come here to exchange trades" his friend across the circle said to him. I was glad he said it instead of me!

The chiropractor, who I now knew was named Bob, started laughing. "Well, it was worth a shot." He paused.

"Ok, sweetie, lets go get that dance."

I smiled at him and looped my arm through his. "You ready then?"

"Let me just grab my drink, and we can go". He plucked his drink off the table as we started making our way for the dance room.

The Local Girl

Most of the dancers were from out of town. Nobody wants to work close to their house, and their hometown. Whether its kids they went to school with, their parents, relatives, or just lack of money, each girl had her own reason for driving for work.

Until we met Dahlia. Dahlia happened to be a long term girl at the club and a local. We didnt talk to her that much, hell we didn't talk to anyone much, but we did use her for a weed connect one Saturday afternoon after work. My friend had made the plans, and I was along for the adventure. This was how I came to find myself zooming through the city streets after a Saturday day shift in the back seat of this girls car.

We were on our way to her weed guys house so we could have something to smoke on the way home.

Luckily I was in the back seat so I didn't have to hold much of the conversation.

"I grew up around here, but all these motha-fucking bitch ass dudes used to pick on me because I was the fat kid." She started laughing "now they all come in and spend their money on me. Fuck around and I'll take their daddy's money too"

She paused.

"Ive been working here for five years now. I do the billboards and the advertisements. I was a little shy at first, but fuck it I need to pay my bills. How funny is it that they're helping me pay them" She laughed again.

My friend was talking to her about how far we were driving everyday for work "we drive an hour and a half each way to get here, but thats nothing compared to the girls who sleep here."

Dahlia chimed in with more long term knowledge "ya, the girls drive here from up north and stay the whole weekend. I mean, the money is good. Well it used to be good. The nights aren't so crazy anymore, shit I used to make thousands in one night but I'm lucky if I make a thousand in one night now. Something fucked is going on with the economy. It has to be, the heavy hitters just aren't spending the same ways that they were."

Now that was interesting, I thought to myself. It made sense though. I had always heard how good this club was, but I had never made the kind of money I heard about. I figured it was because I wasn't offering the same set of services that other girls were offering, so I chalked it up to that. But this tidbit meant that the industry as a whole was suffering. There was something about that fact that made me feel better about myself.

"We're hereee" Dahlia sang out, as we pulled up to a random house. "Come on you both can come in that way if you need something in the future you can come here on your own - if he's cool with it, but we'll at least do introductions today." Dahlia was a burst of energy after working all day.

We all climbed out of the car and headed into what was clearly not a family house. Once inside I was proven right as I noted that they were living more like a trap house rather than one where the kids were outside playing.

"Ayyyyy what's going on Mikey! I brought a couple of the girls with me to grab some bud from you." Dahlia was ahead of us explaining who was with her.

"Yo, next time you need to hit me up before you just show up with random people." I heard what must be Mikey talking in the next room.

Great so he wasn't happy we were there and she said we were strippers. I hated that she told him where we worked, although we couldn't get past it with her especially as she was so flamboyant with where she worked. It just started the introductions out as if we were Those type of girls. At least I wasn't and the lack of money made that day backed me up. I hated to meet someone new and have them judge me, it didnt matter that this was a weed dealer.

We finally made it into the same room as Dahlia and Mikey, and I decided we were not going to be coming back to buy weed without her. The assessment he gave me as I walked into the room made it clear that he put us into a category because of where we worked. I didn't pay attention to the up and down study he made of us and politely entered the conversation

"Hi, I'm Mallory. Nice to meet you." That was it, I was done talking to the creepy weed guy.

"Nice to meet you Mallory, you guys can come here anytime you need to." Mikey said to me as he once again looked me up and down. I'm glad I was in my sweatpants and t-shirt ready to go home, although he made me feel as if I didn't have anything on and I was back at the club.

"Thanks, much appreciated. We have a long ride home so this will make the ride much better." I said.

"Can we grab an eighth, if thats cool." My friend said. Mikey looked at her as if she dampened his mood.

"Sorry to rush it just is a long ride." She said, feeling his unspoken displeasure.

"Oh ya ya, no big deal." He said, although his face did not match his words, we were not going to poke at it.

"Mikey what have you been up to, have you heard from Tommy? Last time I stopped by you and him were beefing. Did you resolve that or what. You've been friends since eighth grade man." Dahlia started talking while Mikey was grabbing our weed.

Clearly they had known each other for quite some time if she was talking to him about eighth grade. Dahlia really did not care to hide what she did from everyone she grew up with. Part of me was impressed and the other part of me thought about her future and what would happen when she wasn't dancing anymore.

Mikey bagged up our weed and my friend passed him the money. "Thanks, Mikey!" Dahlia said, which was followed by

"Thanks"

"Thanks"

From both me and my friend.

"It was nice to meet you Mikey." I said. Damn my politeness, as he thought it was an invitation.

"make sure you give them my number so they can pick up again if they need anything." Mikey said as we headed for the door.

"Will do! I'll call you later!" Dahlia said through the door.

We were already outside waiting for her to unlock her doors.

I climbed in the back as soon as she opened the driver door for me.

"Thank you so much for that!" I said.

"This will definitely make the ride home more tolerable. This was a shit Saturday for money." My friend said.

"You too huh" Dahlia said, "I was thinking it was just me but if you two aren't making money then I wonder if the whole club is feeling it".

The ride back to the club parking lot was much quieter than on the way there. We were all pondering the fact that money was starting to become harder to make. That either meant that there were more girls who were fucking and sucking in the back, or the economy was about to take a nose dive.

We pulled up to the club and Dahlia brought us over to the car. "You girls have a safe drive home. Do you want Mikey's number?"

"I'm all set I think. I probably wouldn't go there without you just because I don't know him that well. Thank you though!"

My friend took a more diplomatic approach and told Dahlia "let me smoke this and then I will let you know".

I dragged myself out of the backseat, damn two door cars, and got out on the passenger side so Dahlia didn't have to get out of her car.

"Thanks again!" I told her before she drove off.

My friend and I looked at each other now that we were alone.

"I don't even know what to make of all that" I said to her as I climbed into the passenger seat. "I could never be in my hometown, dancing for people I went to school with."

"Girl, you and me both. That's why we are here instead of the club in town."

It's Not so Much a Secret Anymore

I was about six months into working at the clubs when I had a bombshell dropped on me, proving that there is no such thing as a secret in a small town.

My family is relatively small, and at the time I would spend time at my aunts house when I wasn't working. She stayed at home during the day with her son, my cousin. Her walls were decorated with photos of the family, mostly of her son or my grandmother, but a few of them included me and my child. Typical family photographs that can be found in all the older relatives homes.

I was sitting on her couch one day when she walked into the living room and said to me what I, naively, thought she would never say.

"I know where you're working." She said very nonchalantly.

I didn't respond to her right away, I was stunned at her words, and was hoping that she didn't really know where. I figured that if I didn't say anything then I lessened the chance of outing myself.

With my silence, she kept going.

"A friend of ours was visiting last week when he saw your photo on the wall." She started. I didn't look up at her.

"He asked me who you were, and I told him that you were my niece. I thought it was weird, but you're cute and he is single" She paused, looking at me to see if I was going to react.

I have learned that there is not just fight or flight, but there is also freeze; and that is just what I did. I froze as I waited for her to continue. My heart was thumping loudly in my chest, I was certain she could here it from where she sat across the room.

"Buy ya know honey, he said the damndest thing. He said that he was almost positive he had seen you when he went out. That you were at a club about an hour and a half away from here."

"Oh?" I said. I tried to not give any emotion in my voice that could potentially be used to implicate me. Although at this point there wasn't much that I could give away.

"He said that you were working there, on a stage. Not as a bottle girl. Not as a bartender." She paused again here, letting her words sink in.

"Now", she went on "I am not going to ask anymore questions and I am not going to be the one to tell the rest of the family but I want you to know I know."

I couldn't tell if she was mad at me, disappointed, or just clearing the air. I didn't look up at her, how could I. I was not happy that she knew, and now I knew I was at risk to have the rest of the family find out, if she could.

"I'm not disappointed, if that is what you're thinking. I just want to make sure that you are careful. Please don't make any stupid choices."

I found the courage to find my voice. "I won't". I answered sheepishly.

I didn't need to say anything else, and she didn't either.

"I had to hide my shock from him, he wasn't sure it was you but he said it certainly looked like you."

"It was probably me. We thought that if we worked far from home that we wouldn't see anyone who we know. It was working up until now." I laughed sardonically to myself. "So much for that."

"I'm not going to ask you anymore questions. In fact I don't even want to know the answers. I wont be the one to tell your mother or Grammy, and if I don't know then I can deny."

"Thank you." I replied to her, sheepishly.

It was one thing to be on a stage and not know anyone. It was entirely another thing to have your family know.

My aunt didn't ask any other questions that night. It may have been just me, but I felt like something had changed. I was probably reading to much into it, I told myself.

Making a Deposit

The stage was where I really shined, perhaps because I didn't have to really talk to anyone. Clearly, I was not built for sales.

Because I did good on the stage, I usually had an extra amount of one dollar bills. I would trade some of them in throughout the night while at the club, but sometimes I didn't.

I spent many a morning sitting on my bed counting out stacks of ones into a denomination that was easily computable. It was usually in stacks of twenty; they sat in nice little piles on the bed which made for an organized count.

I tried to not let them build up to much, as I could have anywhere from five hundred to one thousand dollars in just ones from working two nights.

There are a lot of things that I could buy using cash, where I would offload the ones in place of the larger bills. Places like Walmart, the grocery store, gas station purchases. Bills on the other hand, those had to be paid online or using my bank account.

I hated going to the bank to make deposits. It was always a bunch of ones, with a smaller amount of fives, tens, and of course a slew of twenties.

They may not have been looking at me with suspecting eyes when I went in, but it felt like they were judging me from behind their stations. I know that the first thing that comes to mind when someone sees nothing but ones is "oh where you at the strip club last night", no matter if its a guy or a girl.

Add to this that I was a young girl going into the bank with a stack of ones. They never said anything to me, but I made sure to do as much as possible to make the event as quick as possible.

I would sit home and organize all of the bills to be with the same side facing up, and then further have them facing the same way. I didn't have any money bands, not that it would have saved time as they would have broken them down to count them anyways. I counted and recounted making sure that the amount was spot on. I did not want to have an error on my counting when I got to the teller.

The tellers always seemed to turn their nose up a little bit as I pulled the stack of bills out from my purse. I had pre-filled the deposit ticket out, and laid this on top of the stack of bills that I laid on the counter in front of me.

As soon as they saw this stack their demeanor seemed to cool down a little bit, the air of superiority slightly wafting about them. I always made a point to smile and demurely look at them.

They could think whatever it was they wanted, for all they knew I was a bartender or a waitress. Somehow even though I told this to myself standing at the counter while they counted, it made me feel judged.

I had to remind myself that I was making a deposit that was going to pay my bills, and these snotty women in their bank teller proper clothes were not paying my bills. I didn't have to work the same hours that they did, slaving my life from 9-5.

They may have felt they were better than me, but I had the luxury of freedom. I wasn't beholden to a schedule and I didn't need to wear business minded clothing!

When you are standing in a public place and the person who is supposed to be helping you is judgmental and condescending, it makes the task at hand something that you come to loathe. Even if the teller didn't know what I was doing to earn all of these ones, you could tell that they were making assumptions behind their false smiles

Societies Stigma

People hate strippers. They loathe them in fact. Men will go and spend their hard earned money on their favorite option that night and then turn around and call them a bevy of slews: Slut. Whore. Dirty. Greedy. Money hungry. Sometimes all to their faces, as if they are upset that this is how they're spending their money.

Men love strippers inside of a club, but turn their nose up at the thought of dating one. How could they possibly share their girl with other people?! Fathers weep at the thought of their daughter working in a club, attributing it to bad parenting on their part. Do they not realize that every woman in there is someone's daughter?

And still, it is because of their desire to watch these women that give birth to a strip club! If patrons did not go, there would be no business. Once again, women find a means of making money at the hands of men and those same men degrade the women.

We are damned if we do and damned if we don't.

Women on the other hand, are even worse. Women are jealous creatures and will look down their nose at anyone that does not conform to what they believe is acceptable. There would be some women who came into the club. Sometimes they were lesbians; sometimes they were there to enjoy the atmosphere; sometimes they were there for their own needs. However, the number of women who enter a strip club are the minority.

We live in a capitalist society where the value of a dollar is placed on every single thing we interact with. We sell ourselves to our employer every single day for a paycheck. Our muscles are put to the test in labor intensive jobs. Ours brains are mined for our intellect at white collar jobs.

Why is it wrong for women - and men - to earn a dollar for simply showing a little more than what is shown at the beach? Take a woman who is at the beach in her bikini, give her a drink and play some music and they are guaranteed to dance. Its almost as if they are on a stage, in a club, dancing the same way that a stripper is dancing.

The difference? Depending on the state that someone is in, the stripper on stage will take off some of her clothing.

And this is where people get upset; the exchange of skin for money.

I recently encountered a woman who was irate at the thought that her child's father was dating a stripper. I had been taking a pole dancing class, ironically, and purchased a pole for my home so that I could practice.

By the way, if you have never tried a pole dancing class, it is the best all over body workout that I have ever encountered and is not easy. I highly recommend it if you are trying to get toned up.

I had the pole in my car, broken down into two pieces tucked in my front seat. The intent was to sell it to someone from an online marketplace later in the day. We were going to visit a greenhouse in the western part of the state and so I parked my car at his house for the day.

His ex-girlfriend drove by his house and saw my car. She decided to literally snoop around his house and in my car and happened to see the dance pole in my car.

The litany of messages that he received after seeing the pole in my car was intense for even the strongest person.

This woman who does not have anything of her own and is surviving on the gifts and money received from men she sleeps with had the nerve to degrade someone solely based on the presumption of her stream of income which entails removing clothes. The irony.

It baffles me how women can shame other women so freely. Granted, this woman was irate at the thought of her ex talking to someone other than her, but her immediate reaction was to trash someone being a dancer.

Perhaps I am sensitive to someone trashing strippers, given my secretive past. I hear people make comments about a stripper and inwardly I cringe. Men discuss how they could never date someone like that, or how they have no morals, no values, how they sleep with everyone they encounter, that all a stripper is doing is fucking and sucking in the back.

And 90% of the time they are right.

Epilogue

I wasn't a very good stripper. I excelled on the stage, and failed miserably at lap dances and private rooms.

Sure, I could get them, but if I had one dance everyone else had three if not four. Ones from the stage just did not hit the same way that the twenties or hundreds did from private dances and rooms.

I say all this, because I did not dance for long and I sure as hell did not advertise what I did. I was dancing around 2008, which was before Instagram and Snap Chat really became so popular. I was not posting photos and asking people to come see me the way some of the girls are now.

People did find out about me dancing though. Its hard to keep secrets when you are in a small town. All it takes is for one person to wander out of town and see you, then they tell someone who tells someone who tells someone.

As I faded out of my dancing career within the first year, my mundane, Susan Homemaker life fell out of the gossip spotlight. Time has a way of softening everything, and the gossip mills love to stay current. Those that may have known what I was doing quickly forgot.

My friend, now she did not follow the same path. She went on to keep dancing for another decade. She worked at countless clubs, did numerous bachelor parties, and succumbed to the life that comes with this world.

It saddens me to see the wayward direction our two paths went. There was a point in time where a choice had to be made about whether or not I could stay friends with this person. As I was working a regular 9-5 job, she was still sleeping in after working until sometimes 4 am.

Our schedules clashed.

And then there was the boyfriend.

My boyfriend did not like my friend and did not want me spending time with her.

Notice the irony of this situation, as well as the stereotype of a stripper.

He did not trust me now that I wasn't dancing, to spend time with her.

I would like to believe that he saw the difference in our characters, but he was extremely possessive and controlling and was a whole other book worth of toxic behavior.

Nonetheless, this time period in my life was able to give me a bevy of stories that I can now share with you.

I met a whole bunch of different women, all of them living a different story. I met girls that made their money lying to men, girls who made their money to feed a drug addiction, girls who hated men, girls who had abusive boyfriends, girls that at one point were making the kind of money you see in movies only to have it dry up.

So what was this scene? It was bars filled with women who were in one facet of the sex industry, the oldest known profession to man. I think to one of the many songs that came out in the early 2000's, this one was by Wyclef where he sings about how strippers would rather be up in a club, shaking for a dub, than triple times the money and be able to spend it how they want to. We were in the sex industry, but we weren't supposed to be selling the same thing as prostitutes. We were a fantasy, at least thats what I naively thought when I started.

I wanted out when it became apparent that in order to make money you had to keep up with what was being sold around you. You cannot compete with girls who are selling sex when all you are trying to sell is a fantasy.

Work divulged into nights of watching girls take men into the private dance room right after those same men had just asked me to have sex with them.

I knew what those girls were doing.

I knew that they were not just dancing for them. Once that happens the playing field isn't level anymore and the charade was up. The money that I was once taking home was harder to make.

It also changed the way I saw men. It gave me a general dislike for most of them. When they pay you, they think that they own you. Whether it is one song on the stage, one private dance in the back, or one champagne room, they think that they can do whatever they want with you.

Slowly, you start to value everything in terms of money. You would hear the conversations all the time in the dressing rooms. Girls banter getting ready talking about

"I won't take my bottoms off on stage for less than…"

"I won't sit on a lap for less than…".

"They paid me a lot of money so I let them touch my legs."

When your body is what pays your bills, you start to place a price tag on each part of it. What are your breasts worth? Your nipples? Panties on versus panties off? When you're home, out of the club, you think "why am I going to get dressed up for these people, they're not even paying me." The way the psyche starts to shift is quite fascinating.

I didn't dance for longer than a year. My dancing career happened to fall around the start of the 2008 economic collapse. The money was slowly drying up and girls were pushing their boundaries to keep the lifestyle they had been accustomed to. Eventually it only takes that final solicitation for sex, a blowjob, a handjobs, or finding one more used condom on the floor before it really gets too old.

Frankly, I was tired of seeing the unbridled dark side of the men in society.

I transitioned out of the club scene to a regular job, and it was one of the toughest things I had to do.

Gone were the late nights and days full of freedom. I was back to having to go to work during the day with a set schedule that was non-negotiable.

My paycheck was the hardest thing to get used to. Although I wasn't raking in the money like everyone else, my new paycheck still took all week to make what I had been making in a few nights. Freedom becomes an illusion.

The sacrifice and hard work to make this transition were well worth it. My daughter was getting older and I was going to be a good example of what she should aspire to.

I might have ended up dancing on a stage with limited to no clothes on for money, but that did not mean that I wanted my daughter to grow up with the same goals.

I didn't even want her to have an inkling that this may have been how I made money. Stopping this was not only for myself, but it was also for the mom in me.

Over the years, I worked steadily at integrating back into mainstream work places. People still knew what I had done, and although they didn't talk about it, it was still in the recesses of peoples memories. I remember getting into an argument with the girlfriend of a friend of my boyfriend, and she hurled an attempted insult of how I was once a stripper. Young me laughed and told her to take a long look because at least I could be a stripper unlike her who would get laughed off the stage.

You have to own your past.

Fast forward to today, nearly two decades after my time spent as a dancer and I am not sure that anyone would recall that part of my past. Frankly, with today's sex industry that includes conglomerates like Only Fans, Instagram models, and Craig's list hookups, having danced for a little while isn't the worst of things that I could have done in my past.

Still, it has taken me nearly two decades to sit down and compile this collection of events. Facing a part of your past that you do not like is hard, but again, you have to own your past and not let it own you.